Alcohol
DRINK OR DRUG?

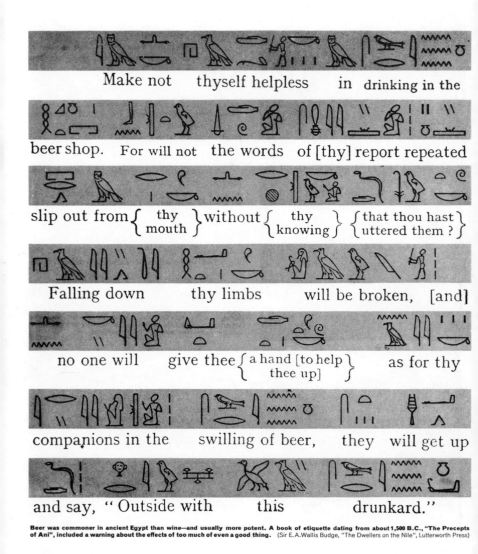

Make not thyself helpless in drinking in the beer shop. For will not the words of [thy] report repeated slip out from { thy mouth } without { thy knowing } { that thou hast uttered them ? } Falling down thy limbs will be broken, [and] no one will give thee { a hand [to help thee up] } as for thy companions in the swilling of beer, they will get up and say, " Outside with this drunkard."

Beer was commoner in ancient Egypt than wine—and usually more potent. A book of etiquette dating from about 1,500 B.C., "The Precepts of Ani", included a warning about the effects of too much of even a good thing. (Sir E. A. Wallis Budge, "The Dwellers on the Nile", Lutterworth Press)

Alcohol
DRINK OR DRUG?

by Margaret O. Hyde

McGRAW-HILL BOOK COMPANY

New York ● St. Louis ● San Francisco ● Düsseldorf ● Johannesburg
● Kuala Lumpur ● London ● Mexico ● Montreal ● New Delhi
● Panama ● Rio de Janeiro ● Singapore ● Syndey ● Tornto

Library of Congress Cataloging in Publication Data

Hyde, Margaret Oldroyd, date.
   Alcohol: drink or drug?

   SUMMARY: Describes the manufacture of major
alcoholic beverages, the problems of alcoholism,
and guidance and research programs for alcoholics.
   Bibliography: p.
   1. Alcoholism—United States. 2. Alcoholics—
Rehabilitation—United States. 3. Liquors.
[1. Alcohol. 2. Alcoholism] I. Title.
[DNLM: 1. Alcohol drinking—Juvenile literature.
2. Alcoholism—Juvenile literature. WM274 H994a
1974]
HV5279.H83   362.2'92   73-17760
ISBN 0–07–031635–X (lib. bdg.)

   345678BPBP7898765

Designed by Marcy J. Katz

For Edwin Y. Hyde, Jr.

Contents

ACKNOWLEDGMENTS

The author wishes to thank the many people who contributed to this book. The following were especially helpful:

Addiction Research Foundation Staff, Toronto, Canada.

Al-Anon Family Groups, New York, New York.

William Alderman, M.D., American Hospital Association.

Russell Brown, M.D., University of Missouri.

Joseph Dolan, OPERATION THRESHOLD, U.S. Jaycees.

Louis Farber, M.D., Texas Research Institute of Mental Science.

Ben R. Forsyth, M.D., University of Vermont College of Medicine.

Paul Garner, National Clearinghouse for Alcohol Information, Department of Health, Education and Welfare.

Gerald Globetti, Ph.D., University of Alabama.

Donald Goodwin, M.D., Washington University.

Milton Gross, M.D., New York Downstate Medical Center.

Institute on Alcohol Abuse and Alcoholism, Department of Health, Education and Welfare.

James Kielty, National Highway Traffic Safety Administration.

Benjamin Kissen, M.D., State University of New York.

Bernard Korol, M.D., St. Louis Veteran's Hospital.

Licensed Beverage Industries, Inc.

Jack Mendelsohn, M.D., Harvard Medical School.

Gail G. Milgram, Ed.D., Rutgers Center for Alcohol Studies.

The National Safety Council.

Mervyn W. Perrine, Ph.D., University of Vermont.

Sally Rothkopf, National Council on Alcoholism.

Drink or Drug of Choice

Certainly, alcohol means many things to many people. It has been called the world's oldest tranquilizer, a tool of the devil, and a servant of man. It may be a food, a food flavor, a medicine, a socializer, an escape route, or serve a long list of other purposes.

Two-thirds of the adult population of the United States drink alcoholic beverages. For most of these individuals, abuse is not a problem. Drinking is generally accepted as part of a way of life and the drinking pattern of most people is responsible and controlled.

However, five percent of the drinking population are alcoholics. For these individuals, alcohol is a drug of choice. It is the most widely used and abused mind drug in many parts of the world. This is true for people of all ages, even though drugs such as marijuana and heroin receive far more publicity. Getting drunk is a "bad trip" for an increasing number of young adults in today's world.

People have been drinking alcoholic beverages since man appeared on the earth, and there is no evidence that they are stopping. In fact, the age at which they begin to drink appears to be lower and the amount they drink seems to be increasing. Adults, young and old, admit alcohol's role in today's culture, and they respect an individual's right to drink responsibly. Along with this should be respect for an individual's decision not to drink.

While this book is not concerned with the individual's choice of whether or not to drink alcoholic beverages, it does deal with the difference between use and abuse. The risk of alcoholism, or the number of alcoholics as related to the number of people who drink cannot be stated with certainty, but some estimates indicate that one of every 15 young people will become an alcoholic.

Nobody really knows why two people may drink the same amount of alcohol with the same frequency and one of them will become an alcoholic, or addict, and the other will not. But there are many theories about the causes of alcoholism and about treatments. Perhaps even more important than treatment is prevention, by knowing how to drink so that one can recognize the danger signals of alcoholism. If one can recognize the clues, he or she may help to prevent the creeping disease known as alcoholism.

When one considers the ancient history of drinking, it is surprising that so many false ideas about the subject exist. For example, here are a few suggested hangover cures: 1) eat as much as you can; 2) take a tranquilizer; 3) take vitamins; 4) drink something that tastes awful; 5) think about something pleasant; 6) ride a bicycle; 7) rest in bed; 8) inhale oxygen; 9) drink large amounts of black coffee. While some of these may take the mind away from the discomfort, none is a cure for a hangover. Some even add a variety of drugs to an already overdrugged body. The surest "cure" is preventive medicine, or drinking responsibly, so that one never gets a hangover.

Alcoholism has been called an "iceberg problem" because so many who suffered from it were afraid or embarrassed to ask for medical help so that the known alcoholics may be as relatively few as the amount of the iceberg that shows above the water. This is about one-eighth of the entire population. Furthermore, many hospitals had no programs for alcoholics. Most admissions of alcoholics were, and many still are, classed as something other than alcoholism.

Many years may pass before the stigma of alcoholism disappears. Before they do, scientists hope to have much more knowledge about what causes this complex disease which involves physical, emotional, social, and behavioral aspects. They hope to learn more about how to reduce the number of drinking problems by increasing positive attitudes about responsible drinking. Certainly, there is a great difference between drinking and drunkenness. There is also a great difference between occasional drunkenness and alcoholism. Alcoholism is a serious public health problem which is being attacked on many fronts.

Alcohol is one of numerous popular beverages which gives great pleasure and causes little or no harm to the majority of people who drink it. In almost all cases, the alcohol that is drunk is ethyl alcohol. By definition, pure ethyl alcohol consists of the chemicals carbon hydrogen and oxygen. Its formula is C_2H_5OH, and it is a colorless liquid with an agreeable odor and a burning taste.

Ethyl alcohol belongs to a family of chemicals, the alcohols, most of which are toxic to the human body even in very small quantities. Since ethyl alcohol passes through the body quickly, it is the least harmful. Methyl alcohol, which has a closely related formula of CH_3OH, can damage the optic nerve, and even kill. While methyl alcohol has many uses such as antifreeze for automobile radiators, as a solvent, as "canned heat," and as a preservative, it is not usable as an alcoholic beverage. Unfortunately, many alcoholics have tried methyl alcohol as a cheap way to quench their thirst for alcohol—with dire results.

Ethyl alcohol, or drinking alcohol, has a wide variety of effects on the human body. The effects may even seem contradictory in the same individual under different circumstances. What happens when alcohol enters the human body and how it acts as a mind drug are described later in this book in some detail.

Alcohol, in the form of beer, wine, and/or liquor is a part of the social life of large numbers of young people whether or not they have involvement with other drugs. Even though it may never be a personal problem, alcohol is a problem for all who care about the welfare of society.

Alcohol-related deaths number in the hundreds of thousands each year in the United States alone. It disables millions. Behind the abstract figures given in volumes of statistics about alcoholics lie millions of stories of lives marred by the misuse of a drug and by a disease that, for many, could have been prevented.

New research is leading the way to answers about disease prevention. But research alone cannot keep alcoholic beverages in the category of "Servant of Man" for all people. The percentage can be greater if more knowledge is available. Learning the facts about alcohol may not be as pleasurable for some as drinking it, but even the knowledge of how beer or wine is made is fascinating. Preventing alcohol-related problems may be far more rewarding for the dedicated in the helping professions than any alcohol or other drug-related high.

Alcohol
Through
the Years

Long before man appeared on earth, the kind of alcohol used in modern beverages was in existence. Since it results from a process known as fermentation and involves organisms that are extremely common, this is not surprising. These organisms, small plants known as yeast, are familiar to those who bake their own bread.

Yeast reacting with tree sap, fruit, berries, honey, the stems of flowers or plants probably made the first beer and wine without the help of man. Through the years and even today, these reactions take place naturally and traces of alcohol may be found in unusual places. For example, there may be some in rain and snow since alcohol evaporates so easily from where it is made naturally on the earth.

Early man probably discovered the effects of drinking alcoholic beverages after some water, plant sugars, and yeast reacted accidentally. Such a man probably lived about 1 or 2 million years ago when humans first appeared on earth. He did not need to know what was happening to the sugar or the meaning of fermentation, but he certainly felt what was happening to him.

Men who have studied the history of alcoholic beverages believe that the first one man knew was probably mead, a wine that is produced when honey ferments. Mead wine is not common today, but some scientists at Cornell University, Ithaca, New York, are producing it on an experimental basis. The wine has a lemon color, mild flavor, and is slightly carbonated. Aging takes from 2 to 6 years. Perhaps mead wine will be "rediscovered" and take a popular place among the fruit wines of today.

Fermented grain can become beer or liquor. The latter did not appear until man learned how to distill alcohol on a large scale sometime in the fifteenth century. Before then, beer and wine were the beverages which played a large part in the lives of most people around the world.

According to one story, the first wine was discovered in a very interesting way. One of the culture heroes of Persian mythology, King Jemsheed, or Jamshid, was thought to be very fond of grapes. It was the custom to store grapes in jars so that through the year he would have grapes to eat whenever he pleased. One time, he discovered that the grapes in one of the jars were no longer sweet. He did not realize it, but they had fermented.

The king believed that the liquid in the jar containing the spoiled grapes was poison and had the jar so labeled. About that time, one of the ladies in the harem of King Jemsheed was suffering from nervous headaches. She attempted to commit suicide rather than suffer from the pain and her choice of method was to drink from the jar labeled poison. One can guess what happened. Rather than dying, she became intoxicated by what was actually wine, she fell asleep, and later awakened feeling better. The lady continued sipping from the jar from time to time until it was empty. Although she may have been the first alcoholic—even in fiction—and she may have had unpleasant experiences as well as comfort from the wine, what happened to her was a surprise to the people who discovered her secret. She was forced to communicate her experiences to the king. As a result, a quantity of wine was made, and Jemsheed drank with the members of his court and thoroughly enjoyed the new beverage. This is the story of the origin of wine according to authorities of Persian history.

Not everyone agrees as to the details of how wine was discovered, but it was probably discovered by accident and the accident was probably a happy one for those who used the new beverage in moderation.

No matter when or where alcoholic beverages were discovered, the chemistry of fermentation is much the same, as it was before man appeared on the earth. Imagine some fruit lying in a field in a dark, damp place. Or imagine some grain in similar conditions. Certain enzymes, chemicals in the natural fruit or grain, change the starch or sugar into a form that can be digested by the microscopic plants which you know as yeast.

If you are interested in the chemical change, here is the equation for the changing of grain starch into malt sugar or maltose:

$$2(C_6H_{10}O_5)_x + H_2O \xrightarrow{\text{enzyme}} xC_{12}H_{22}O_{11}$$

Starch + water   yields malt sugar

Now, another reaction takes place. The maltose changes to another form of sugar known as glucose:

$$C_{12}H_{22}O_{11} + H_2O \longrightarrow 2C_6H_{12}O_6$$

Maltose or sucrose + water yields glucose

Sucrose is table sugar, and a form of glucose is commonly used in intravenous injections after surgery and in certain illnesses. All of this seems a long way from alcoholic beverages, but it is part of a natural process.

Now the yeast comes into action. Yeast can be purchased in grocery stores in small squares. It is also used to start the decaying action in septic tanks where these microscopic one-cell plants play a part in breaking down waste matter.

Yeast changes sugar, or ferments it, so that the carbon, oxygen, and hydrogen atoms are rearranged in the form of ethyl alcohol.

$$C_6H_{12}O_6 \xrightarrow{\text{zymase from yeast}} 2C_2H_5OH + 2CO_2$$

Glucose yields ethyl alcohol + carbon dioxide

The carbon dioxide which forms is responsible for the popping of champagne corks, the bubbles in a number of kinds of wine, and the "head" on a glass of beer.

No matter what the original source of ethyl alcohol, be it a form of starch or sugar, the chemical change takes place so that in the final product there is carbon dioxide which may escape into the air or be contained with the beverage.

The first alcoholic beverages were probably not very palatable. The same is true of many today. Even alcoholics have been known to say that they hate the taste of the "stuff." Many people learn to enjoy the taste of such beverages for social reasons. And there is a wide distance from the worst to the best as well as a wide variation in individual taste.

Beverage alcohol contains many things besides ethyl alcohol, even when it is found in nature. But no matter how an alcoholic drink is formed; no matter if one considers an ancient wine or a modern one; or no matter if one considers beer, liquor, or any other form the process known as fermentation is involved. The importance of this process and man's use of it has changed the course of history around the world.

Very, very long ago, according to some authorities, early mankind probably changed a life style of roaming the land to one of farming because of having to wait for grapes to mature. The grapes for wine may have been the first farm crop. Certainly, the story of alcohol is woven throughout history in many ways, but the history of its early usage is obscure. It is well known that scientists have unearthed pottery in Mesopotamia which shows scenes of fermentation and this pottery has been dated as far back as 4200 B.C.

The mood changing and pain-relieving effects have been recorded in many places in early history. According to Biblical history, Noah planted a vineyard, made wine from grapes, and "became drunken." Noah was just ten generations after Adam. On one medical papyrus which is dated about 3,500 years ago, there are 39 prescriptions for the use of beer and wine.

One ancient prescription is of special interest because of its content and the directions. The following was translated from the cuneiform on a Sumerian tablet of about 4,000 years ago: "Seed of the carpenter plants; gum resin of markazi; thyme; pulverize; dissolve in beer; let the man drink." Mark Keller, a research specialist in documentation at the Center of Alcohol Studies, Rutgers University, New Jersey, comments on this prescription in the following manner: "I have no idea what effects the plant material in this compound had on the patient. It seems that he probably got relief from his pain if he faithfully followed the doctor's directions of 'let the man drink.'"

The peoples of many early civilizations were well acquainted with alcoholic beverages. Bacchus, the classical Greek god of wine, is so famous that the word "bacchant" is used in the English language to mean a "drunken reveler" or "liking alcoholic beverages." There are records of common use in Babylonia, Chaldea, Egypt, Greece, Rome, and other countries. Perhaps this was partly due to the availability of these drinks and to the fact that they were probably less apt to carry disease than the water which was available for drinking in early times.

Everyday use of wine and beer was so common in many cultures that drunkenness and the abuse of alcohol were recognized as problems. This was true of the ancient Greeks, Chinese, Persians, Indians, and other peoples. The exact dates of the origin of wine-making are not known for all of these, but it is certain that the Chinese knew how to make wine for more than 2,000 years before Christ.

The oldest mind drug, alcohol, was not used by the Moslems for it is forbidden by the Koran. It has been suggested that its use was forbidden in an effort to prevent the thirst for water which follows the drinking of alcohol. Such thirst obviously would be undesirable in the water-scarce areas where most Moslems dwell. But no one knows whether such an idea is true. They were not the only ancient peoples who did not drink alcoholic beverages because of religious principles. The Brahmins in India and adherents to Buddhism kept multitudes of followers from drinking, although there was a wine of very short fermentation that was acceptable to Buddhists.

Although drunkenness was not only given approval but admired in some cultures, moderation was most commonly encouraged and the temperance movement had some advocates as long as 3,000 years ago, and perhaps even before this. Through the years, there were attempts by teachers and governments to reform or control excessive drinking among those who used alcohol to induce light-headedness whenever they wished.

Many think of the Puritans in America as totally abstaining from alcoholic beverages, but such was not the case. The Puritans are said to have chosen Plymouth Rock as a landing place because their supply of food and beer was running low. Because of this, they could not wait to find a better harbor. Exactly how large a part the lack of beer played in the location of the landing of the Pilgrims cannot be fully determined, but the diary of a passenger on the Mayflower reads: "We could not take time for further search or consideration; our victuals being much spent especially our beere. . ." This diary was to find its place in the Library of Congress of the United States.

Beer was probably the first imported alcoholic beverage in the United States, but rum played an important part in the lives of the early Colonists. Rum production had started in the West Indies by 1650 and much found its way to the early settlers.

In less than a few hundred years before the Puritans arrived in America, most alcoholic beverages contained no more than 14% alcohol. This is easy to understand when one knows that fermentation does not continue naturally until the sugar supply is exhausted. When the amount of alcohol increases, the activity of the yeast organisms is slowed. When the amount of alcohol in the brew reaches 14%, the yeast no longer carries on its living process.

The discovery of distillation made possible a stronger type of spirit or beverage. While distillation may have been known in antiquity, and Aristotle mentions purifying sea water by evaporation and producing a "spirit" from wine, many authorities credit an alchemist as the first true distiller. This Greek or Egyptian was said to boil some wine in a crude still in his effort to transmute a base metal into gold. A beer made by distilling rice was known to the ancient Chinese. But the modern history of distillation begins about the tenth century with an Arabian alchemist. Perhaps this is why the Arabian word for still, "alembic," is still used in some countries. The word "alcohol" was introduced about this time, too.

The alcoholic beverage known as spirit of wine became popular in Europe during the fifteenth century. This was more potent than ordinary wine since distillation was involved in its making.

By distillation, beverages containing as much as, and sometimes more than, 50% alcohol could be made. The distillation of alcohol follows the same basic principle of distillation as that of other liquids. When heat is applied, so that the boiling point is reached, the vapor is caught, cooled, and condensed or returned to liquid form. In the case of ethyl alcohol, the boiling point is 176°F. This is somewhat lower than the 212°F at which water boils.

All of the alcohol may be separated from an original liquid by boiling. The still is an apparatus used to collect the alcoholic vapors to prevent them from escaping into the air. The drops of liquid which form when the gas condenses are of very high purity. In theory, distilling alcohol is quite simple; distilling it to produce a tasty alcoholic beverage is, indeed, an art.

In far parts of the world and in various centuries, spirits known as the "water of life" were used. Various names were given to this drink such as aquavit (akvavit)—which is still the national beverage of the Scandinavian countries—*aqua vitae, eau de vie,* and *uisgebeatha* or *uisebaugh.* The latter are names used in early centuries by the Celts of Scotia or Scotland. *Usige veatha* was the popular name in Ireland.

Aqua vitae was used as medicine on a large scale soon after it was discovered. In surgery, it was the best anesthetic available at the time. It replaced wine in many medicinal prescriptions, and some early users thought it might be the long-sought-after philosopher's stone or "fountain of youth." Actually, aqua vitae did not rejuvenate the body nor did it cure the many diseases for which it was prescribed, but it did reduce emotional stress. From the early use of distilled spirits in the fifteenth and sixteenth centuries to modern times, alcohol has had its place in medicine. This will be discussed in greater detail later in this book.

Some of the early references to aqua vitae are especially interesting. For example, one of the earliest is an entry made, in 1494, in the Scottish Exchequer Rolls. Here is recorded: "8 bolls of malt to Friar John Cor wherewith to make Aquavitiae." Later references occur from time to time. For example, in September of 1506, there was a prescription recorded for "Aqua Vite to the Kings Ills." One early reference got into the records in a rather strange way. A man was accused of the crime for breaking into a private house and of assault during which he was said to have knocked over some "Aquavitie." Certainly, this form of distilled beverage was used long before the Pilgrims landed.

While the distilled alcoholic beverage, rum,

had its part in the life of the Puritans, and some of the other forms of strong alcoholic drinks were used, moderation was urged and drunkenness was sometimes punished by fines, whipping, and confinement in the stocks.

In the Virginia Colony, in the year 1619, excessive drinking was so common that a law was passed with the following penalties: Anyone found drunk for the first time was to be privately reproved by the clergy; the second time, the reproof would be public; and the third time, the person was to "lye in halter" for 12 hours and pay a fine. In Virginia, as in many other places, it was not the use of alcoholic beverage that was unacceptable, but the abuse or drinking to excess.

For the early English Colonists in America, beer was a table drink, much as water is for many Americans today. It was given to the children rather than water which they thought to be impure.

The stories about American Indians and "firewater" are being reexamined today. Two social scientists, Craig MacAndrew and Robert B. Edgerton of the University of California at Los Angeles, have recently published a book about drunken comportment in which they reject the legend that the North American Indian became wildly savage when introduced to alcoholic beverages. They claim that more typical behavior on the part of American Indians was caution, with the eldest of the tribe being coaxed to sample the drink. In many cases, the alcohol had a tranquilizing effect, much as it does with people in near and far parts of the world today.

The so-called firewater is said to have played a part in the naming of Manhattan. When Henry Hudson sailed the *Half Moon* into the mouth of the Hudson River, he stopped at the heavily wooded, large, flat island where he saw some natives fishing. Wanting to know something about where the river led, he and some of his crew went ashore to see what they could learn through the use of sign language. He took with him a cask of gin, for it was the custom in Holland to begin all business and all discussions with friends and strangers by joining together in a round of drinks. Anything less would have been impolite.

Although the Indians who were fishing at what is now Battery Park in Manhattan had never tasted gin, they liked it. They asked for more, and the party was a pleasant one. Later, the Indians decided to name that deserted island in honor of the party, the place where they had such a good time, so they called it "Mana-hachta-nienk." This later became Manhattan which was far easier for the white man to pronounce.

While reports are mixed as to the reactions of Indians throughout the United States when given liquor, it is probably true that both the white frontiersmen and the native Indians indulged in varying degrees of drinking, ranging from moderation to excess.

At one time, rum played such an important part in the economy of New England and New York that it is credited with a part in instigating the American Revolution. There was a vicious triangle of trading rum, molasses, and slaves. Merchants sent ships from North America, especially from Massachusetts and Rhode Island, to the Guinea Coast of Africa where slaves were purchased from native blacks. The slaves were taken to the West Indies where there was little money but plenty of molasses. The molasses, which paid for the slaves, was imported by New Englanders who distilled it into rum. Some of the rum was then exported. England's Sugar and Molasses Act which imposed "taxation without representation" was a source of much unrest among the Colonists. The famous Boston Tea Party involved more than tea.

Rum was so popular during the Revolutionary War that it was considered essential to the well-being of the troops, and a regular rum ration was dealt to the soldiers.

About the time of the American Revolution, whiskey appeared in the mountainous sections of Pennsylvania, Maryland, and North Carolina. Here, rye, barley, and corn were distilled in mountain cabins and some of the whiskey found its way into army camps where there was a shortage of rum. Dr. Benjamin Rush, Surgeon General of the Continental Middle Army, published a paper in 1789 in which he made it clear that he felt that liquor was bad for people and that its curative powers had been exaggerated. He is considered one of the first of the American temperance movement.

The temperance movement sprang in great part from the alcoholic excesses in England during the Industrial Revolution. Gin was introduced into England in the early seventeenth century by British soldiers returning from wars in the Low Countries. They found that gin gave them "Dutch courage" to endure the long campaign. English brewers learned to make gin from English grain, and the consumption of gin rose rapidly about this time. Later, the consumption was slowed somewhat by a duty placed on gin.

Between 1700 and 1750, there was a steady stream of immigrants into London. The working classes prospered and they were able to afford gin which they enjoyed after a long working day. Although gin was frowned upon by some of the middle class who felt it increased the crime rate, many of these people left the city for places in the country. They associated gin drinking with the lower classes, but accepted beer, although beer was still the drink of choice for many of the working class.

Then there was a strange turn of events. Coffee and tea began to take the place of alcoholic beverages toward the end of the eighteenth century in England. About 90% of the families drank tea twice a day. But tea was blamed equally with gin for harming the lives of the common people. At the same time, beer drinking was still considered a virtue. The upper classes drank wine and brandy.

The drinking patterns in America changed during these centuries. Before 1700, drinking was largely family-centered and controlled. It consisted mostly of wine and beer. During the eighteenth century, liquor that was distilled and contained a higher alcoholic content became increasingly popular. There was excessive drinking and, along with this, there was more concern about the problems caused by too much drinking. Moderation was encouraged.

Actually, the temperance movement began with encouragement of moderation rather than abstinence. In the early part of the nineteenth century, the temperance movement changed in concept and goal. By 1910, the movement was very strong, and national prohibition began in the United States in 1919. Known as the "Noble Experiment," it did not succeed in stamping out alcoholism or excessive drinking. While prohibition prevented many from coming in contact with alcohol, it brought those who insisted on drinking in contact with criminals and helped

the criminals to flourish. Many credit the Prohibition Era with damaging respect for policemen who were expected to enforce laws which
many believed took away their rights. On the
other hand, it did hide, at least from public view,
the many acts of destructive behavior that were
common in those days.

Alcoholics who existed during the years of
Prohibition, and there were many, were treated
for other diseases. Since alcoholism was not
supposed to exist, there could be no research on
the subject.

Even though the legal prohibition of alcohol
in the United States was defeated in 1932, it did
leave a change in American attitudes toward
drinking which still affects the thinking of many
people today. For some, this may be a good
thing; for others, a very bad problem. Certainly,
there are many struggles between the "wets"
and the "drys" today, several decades after the
repeal of the law. Unfortunately, many physi-
cians, as well as people in general, still view the
alcoholic in a punitive way.

The differences in feelings about alcohol
depend largely on one's lack of experience or
on one's bad or good experiences with this mind
drug. Feelings about drinking are also influenced largely by parental drinking habits and
attitudes. Alcoholic use is a learned behavior for
most people, and it is not surprising to find that
responsible drinking habits tend to be passed

on from one generation to the next. As discussed later, most alcoholics come from families where alcohol is either strictly forbidden or where parents are alcoholics.

But what does drinking in moderation do to the human body? How does the body react when drinking is occasional and part of a social setting?

Alcohol and the Human Body

Does the drinking of alcoholic beverages meet some deep and fundamental need in people, or is it just a dangerous way to relax? Aside from the moral aspects of drinking, what are the true facts of what alcohol can do to the human body? What does it do when used in moderation? What happens when a person becomes an alcoholic or addict?

Both alcohol and heroin can, and should, be classed as drugs, for they are chemicals that can alter the function and structure of living tissue. Alcohol addiction is completely destructive to the human mind, while heroin addiction is not. However, most users of alcohol do not become addicted to their drug of choice, while most users of heroin do.

Of the 90 million people in the United States who drink, it is estimated that between 5 and 10 million suffer severely from too much alcohol. These people are alcohol abusers or alcoholics. Some alcoholics become so dependent on alcohol that they are considered addicts.

Opinions on the effect of alcohol on the human body vary from encouraging its use as a medicine to a recent statement in *Licit and Illicit Drugs,* by Edward M. Brecher and the editors of *Consumer Reports* in which they state, "The amount of damage done to the human mind alone, as measured by mental hospital admissions, vastly exceeds the mental harm done by all the other psychoactive drugs put together." Much depends on the individual case.

First consider what alcohol does to the body of a person who drinks only occasionally. How does the healthy body eliminate its alcohol poison? Follow the path of a drink as it enters the human body through the mouth. In the stomach, only about 20% of the alcohol is absorbed, and that absorption takes place slowly even though the alcohol does not have to be digested before the body can use it. As with other foods, most of the absorption into the bloodstream takes place from the walls of the intestine. In the case of alcohol, this happens rapidly and completely until all of the alcohol has been removed from the intestinal tract.

Compare two people who drink the same amount of alcohol. One becomes intoxicated; the other does not. What factors influence the rate at which the alcohol is absorbed into their blood? One of these is the amount of food in the stomach. It is well known that drinking when the stomach is empty can produce a much greater effect on the body than when food is present. Eating a meal before drinking may well reduce the peak alcohol level as much as one half. Fatty foods are known to delay the effect of drinking. Milk and cream have often been used as a buffer by people who feel they must drink in a social situation but who want to keep their thinking clear. In general, the human body can usually handle a drink containing one ounce of alcohol per hour.

In the case of the two people who are drinking equal amounts of alcohol, one drink contains a carbonated beverage and one does not. The one mixed with a carbonated beverage will travel through the stomach with greater speed than the drink which does not contain carbon dioxide. If all other factors were the same, drinking equal amounts of alcohol would have more effect on the person who drank it mixed with a carbonated beverage.

Suppose one drinker weighs more than the other. His body can handle the alcohol more easily. For example, a person who weighs 150 pounds could drink more in the same amount of time than a person weighing 100 pounds for the same change of feeling, if all other factors were equal. One exception to this is the case of an obese person. Fat tissue cannot dissolve its share of alcohol because of its low water content. Fat drinkers are more apt to feel the effects of alcohol than lean persons having the same body weight. The effect of alcohol or concentration in the blood may well vary with the weight of the individual.

The effect of alcohol on the human body is not felt until the alcohol reaches the bloodstream. Even though no effects may be felt where the drink is 5-1/2 ounces of ordinary wine, the concentration of alcohol in the blood would be 0.03% and the time required for most of this alcohol to leave the body would be 2 hours in the person weighing 150 pounds.

In general, the more slowly the alcohol passes from the digestive tract into the bloodstream, the less effect it has on the drinker. This is true because the body is working steadily to remove the drug.

Suppose the two drinkers are experimenting with a beverage with a very high alcohol content. There may be some surprising results.

In one person, the high alcohol content irritates the pyloric valve, a gateway that opens and closes between the stomach and small intestine. This irritation closes the valve and slows the speed with which the highly concentrated drink passes into the small intestine. Now the alcohol content in the stomach is becoming more concentrated, and the valve goes into spasms. This is a reaction that is familiar to many people. The drinker becomes nauseous and vomits. As a result, his body is actually protected from the amount of alcohol that would normally go into the bloodstream and result in intoxication.

In the other person in the experiment, the alcohol passes quickly into the intestines. Here millions of microscopic blood vessels absorb the alcohol, and larger blood vessels carry it to the liver where it is mixed with blood from the hepatic artery. This mixture goes to the right side of the heart and to the lungs along with blood which has returned from all other parts of the body. It travels with the blood returning from the lungs to the left side of the heart and then throughout the body. The alcohol in the blood exerts its most immediate influence on the brain. The drinker feels relaxed and is less concerned with minor irritations. He has a feeling of warmth although actually his body temperature is lowered.

While small amounts of alcohol may appear to be a stimulant, generally speaking, alcohol is a depressant. Some of the confusion exists because alcohol causes the capillaries, which carry blood just beneath the surface of the skin, to become dilated and more blood travels through them. This causes a flushed skin and a warm feeling. This feeling is limited to the skin area, and the drinker actually is not warmed since much internal heat is taken from his other organs to his skin.

In general, after three drinks a person's coordination is impaired, and there is an increasing unsteadiness in his ability to stand or walk. Cells in the cerebral cortex, or the outer layer of the brain, are affected so the ability to think and to learn is altered. While a small amount of alcohol has a tranquilizing effect for most people, larger amounts depress the highly developed brain centers which store learned behavior.

Some interesting studies have been made in connection with arguments about whether or not people can perform better after drinking a moderate amount of alcoholic beverage. Suppose people are tested for ability to associate words or give illustrations after they have a few drinks, and this ability is compared with their performance when they have had no alcohol. Tests showed some performed better after a single drink than before. In another case, some very intelligent people were given between 2 and 6 ounces of whiskey and asked to solve some complicated problems in logic. They, too, performed better. Different reactions seem to take place in different parts of the brain, some being stimulated while others are depressed.

Awareness of cues, such as noticing a driver who suddenly comes toward a drinker's car, is less acute. So is ability to perceive a total situation; ability to think in relation to the overall picture is reduced.

Inhibitions are lost, and the drinker may talk more freely, feel aggressive, or even depressed. Alcohol acts on the brain much like an anesthetic. With increased amounts of alcohol, the brain "goes to sleep"; there is a loss of control of areas which produce sensory perception and judgment is greatly impaired. If the amount of alcohol level increases enough, it anesthetizes the brain and coma or death may result.

Obviously, it is difficult, if not impossible, to determine how much one can drink without feeling the effects or showing them. The amount which the body can handle efficiently depends on many factors, including the amount of fat in a person's body, the time during which a given amount is consumed, the health of the person, the conditions under which a person is drinking, and many others. What can be drunk with little effect one day, may cause drunkenness on another.

Measures of the amount of alcohol in the blood do seem to fall in line to some extent with a person's behavior. Beginning at about .05 percent, a person's behavior differs from his normal behavior; at .10 percent, speech becomes slurred and equilibrium uncertain; at .10 percent, most states consider the person unfit to drive a car; and at increasing levels, a person proceeds from a staggering gait to unconsciousness. Fortunately, practically all people become unconscious before they can drink themselves to death at one occasion, but there have been reports of people literally drinking themselves to death in contests. In such cases, alcohol level in the blood might reach .50 percent. This is certainly a reason to store alcohol out of the reach of children.

What do you think alcohol does to one's sense

of humor? Although people have laughed at drunks through the years, the observers might better feel sorry for them, especially for the alcoholics who cannot bring themselves to stop drinking. On the other hand, tests have been made on groups of young men in which one had a small amount of alcohol and the other had none. The drinkers seemed to find cartoons depicting humor funnier than the control group. Exactly why, no one knows.

Fantasy production, or the imagining of non-existent situations, has been widely tested in people who were given alcohol through a test known as the Thematic Apperception Test (TAT). In this test, the subject is shown a picture which represents a scene or situation and is asked to tell a story about the characters shown in the picture. Stories by those who had high alcohol levels in their blood had themes of physical violence, aggression, and sex more often than those in the control group. There were fewer concerns with time, fear, and anxiety.

Tests measuring speed and accuracy showed that a person who had several drinks tended to work through a complicated test in a hurry but made more mistakes than he would normally. Subjects believed they were very accurate, and found it difficult to believe they had erred so often. This feeling of imagined superiority after drinking is a familiar one.

The effect of alcohol on a person's sex experiences is not well understood, although the effect varies somewhat with the individual. For example, a person who lacks confidence, feels guilty about sex, or has other restraints may find that a moderate amount of alcohol increases ability to participate in sexual activity.

On the other hand, even though drinking may make many people feel more amorous, the truth was expressed by Shakespeare's famous line, "Drink provokes the desire, but taketh away the performance." Scientific studies with lower forms of animal life confirm this, but only tentative conclusions have been drawn with humans. It may be that alcohol or another drug increases interest in sex in a person who is already motivated in that direction. In some cases, what a person expects plays a large part.

Sleep is another activity which is disturbed by the intake of alcohol. Here, too, the short-term effect on central nervous system and the brain in particular depends on the amount of alcohol in the blood. Several ounces of alcohol before bedtime can deprive a person of the normal amount of dreaming sleep, a part of the sleep pattern which is necessary for normal emotional life during the daytime. After a drinking bout, one is apt to feel irritable, tired and anxious the following day, partly because of the lack of the dreaming (REM) stage of sleep. The dreaming stage of sleep is determined when REM takes place. Scientists in many dream laboratories have recorded rapid eye movements during this period.

Many of the other effects of short term, or occasional heavy, drinking are well known. Not only is there an intoxicating effect on the brain, with disturbance in sleep pattern, but headache, nausea, and a variety of aches and pains that are part of the famous "hangover." Some authorities believe that these are a form of acute withdrawal from the alcohol, even in people who do not drink regularly.

From the time alcohol enters the blood, the process of eliminating it begins. Some is excreted from the lungs, kidneys, and sweat glands. The alcohol which is evaporated as one breathes out is the cause of "alcohol breath." Some alcohol passes in the urine unchanged in form. But about 90 percent of the alcohol is changed in the liver by a process known as oxidation. Oxygen from the air which one breathes combines with the alcohol in the body to form new compounds and release energy. In this sense, alcohol is somewhat like food. Although it need not be digested to be used, a gram of alcohol produces about 7 calories, and an ounce of whiskey yields about 75 calories. The following contain about 105 calories each: 8 ounces of beer, 1-1/2 ounces of gin; 1-1/2 ounces of rum; 1-1/2 ounces of whiskey; 2

ounces of port. Two ounces of sherry produces about 76 calories.

The calories supplied by alcohol often are called "empty calories" since they do not supply the body with vitamins, minerals, and other nutrients that are needed. In the case of short-term effects, this loss is not so important as it is in the case of the alcoholic.

The change from alcohol to carbon dioxide and water which are its final products in the body includes a number of steps. Alcohol is first converted to a substance called acetaldehyde, a chemical which is much more toxic to the body than the ethyl alcohol. Fortunately, the body quickly converts acetaldehyde to a form of acetate which is practically harmless. Only a very small amount of acetaldehyde remains in the body of the moderate drinker. The acetate is oxidized to become carbon dioxide and water.

The faster the drug, alcohol, is eliminated from the body, the less harm it does. People have many home remedies for speeding the process which they think of as sobering. Black coffee is one of the most popular, although it probably has value only in helping a drunken person to stay awake, not in sobering him or her. Time is the best remedy for too much alcohol.

Dr. Cleamond D. Eskelson and his colleagues at the Veterans Administration Hospital in Tucson, Arizona, are searching for a way of speeding sobriety after excessive alcohol intake. They gave rats large amounts of certain vitamins and fructose, the sugar found in honey, after the rats had a known intake of alcohol. They noted that the blood alcohol level decreased more rapidly than in rats which were not given these substances. The chemicals chosen for the experiment were selected because they are used by some of the enzymes in the body to convert alcohol into chemical forms which do not affect the brain. The chemical, sodium acetate, has been shown to be of value in inhibiting alcohol absorption in animals when given to them at the same time as an oral dose of alcohol. For example, the amount of alcohol given is usually enough to keep the rats drunk for 2 to 3 hours. But if sodium acetate is given, the blood alcohol levels never attain the level which was considered that necessary for intoxication.

No one knows whether these experiments will lead to a "sober" pill that partygoers can take before driving home or not, but such experiments may prove to be very valuable in helping to reduce the alcohol levels of people who must drive after drinking or who are suffering from too much alcohol in their bodies. One thing is certain, the old, common methods do not accomplish this.

A healthy liver is of considerable value, but unfortunately this is not something one can acquire. On the other hand, one can help to prevent liver damage by avoiding too much drinking. The liver is a famous organ in relation to alcohol and alcohol problems. The enzymes which are necessary to change acetaldehyde to acetate are produced by the liver. The amount of alcohol that the body can handle depends on the amount of "working liver."

While there seems to be a temporary inflammation and swelling of the liver during severe intoxication, permanent damage is associated with long-term drinking. This and other problems of the alcoholic will be discussed in a later section of this book.

Increased frequency of urination is another effect of drinking alcoholic beverages. Part of this is due to a greater intake of water, and to a response of the pituitary gland in the head which plays a part in controlling the output of urine. Increased frequency of urination may last for several hours. Alcoholic beverages do not dehydrate the body, but they do cause temporary redistribution of water in the body. The thirst which is well known by those who drink more than moderate amounts, is due to the shifting of water from inside to the outside of body cells.

Sometimes a person seems to react abnormally to small amounts of alcohol. A drink that would normally have little effect may produce intoxication if a person has taken another drug, such as a tranquilizer, before drinking. Take the case of Sue who attended a formal gathering where many dignitaries were present. She wanted to appear at her best, so she accepted just one drink. While dinner was being served, Sue grew very sleepy and was very embarrassed later when she discovered she had fallen asleep in a chair after dinner while someone was talking to her. Normally, Sue would have had little reaction from a single drink, but earlier in the day she had taken some tranquilizers which her doctor prescribed for times of tension. The two drugs, the tranquilizers and the alcohol, had a synergistic effect, one greater than the sum of two.

Alcohol and barbituates are particularly dangerous in combination. Many people have died from doses of these drugs which separately would have produced only deep sedation.

The desire to alter one's mood from time to time is considered normal, natural, and desirable for human beings. Whether or not this is done by the participation in sports, religious observances, sex, travel, drugs, or some other way depends on the individual, the availability, and the occasion. The use of mind-changing drugs for altering mood seems to be almost universal and has been occurring throughout recorded history in almost all societies. In many, the drug of choice has been, and is, alcohol.

While many people drink for reasons other than obtaining a "high" or a good feeling, almost all wish to avoid the sick feeling, the hangover, and the physical damage which comes from crossing the borderline between moderate and heavy drinking.

Beer

Just what is beer? The word beer is used to describe a number of alcoholic beverages, all of which are made from germinated grains such as barley or other starchy cereals, and they are flavored with hops for better taste. Hops are the dried, ripe cones of the female flowers of a twining plant that is scientifically a member of the genus Humulus.

The beer which is most common today is not the beer referred to in an earlier chapter in connection with the Pilgrims. The Pilgrims' beer was really ale, which is usually fuller-bodied or richer in consistency and more bitter than the beer which is common in America today. The biggest difference between them is that ale is fermented at a higher temperature and the yeast remains at the top of the brew.

Lager beer, the more common form, was introduced into America about 1840 by the German immigrants who made St. Louis, Milwaukee, and Cincinnati world-famous brewing centers. All American beers are lager beers, which are characteristically bright, clear, and light-bodied.

Stout is a very dark form of beer with a strong malt flavor and a sweet taste.

Porter is a type of ale which has a very heavy foam. It is sweeter than regular ale and not quite as strong in alcoholic content as stout.

Bock beer is a special brew of dark, sweet

beer. It is prepared in the winter and is drunk for about a period of 6 weeks to celebrate the arrival of spring.

Pilsner is used on the labels of many light beers in various parts of the world, although it originally came from a place called Pilsen in Czechoslovakia. It is a form of lager beer.

Few people think of sake, a drink that originated in Japan as a beer, but because it is made from rice, it is considered in this class. Sake is a refermented brew, so it contains a higher alcoholic content (14 to 16% by volume) than most beers.

In general, beer varies in its alcoholic content from as little as 1% to as much as 8%, but most all beers consumed today contain between 3% to 4% alcohol by weight and 4% to 5% alcohol by volume. When compared with table wines which contain about 12% alcohol and hard liquors with 40% to 50% alcohol, beers seem quite harmless indeed. But since beers are enjoyed by so many people and are comparatively cheap, they are often drunk in quantities which can produce drunkenness.

While most people are enjoying their beer drinking without harm, some are becoming addicted to the alcohol in their beer. Others are finding that a "six pack" contains enough alcohol to cause the drinker to be legally classed as a drunken driver. In general, beer plays a positive part in the lives of the many millions of people who slake their thirst with as much as 1.6 billions of gallons of beer a year.

Next to water, beer is probably the most popular drink in the world. It is having a recent surge in popularity, but it always has been a favorite drink.

Brewers in medieval times were often bakers, since yeast was used in both products. Many colleges, monasteries, and cities had their own breweries. Some are very old; one famous beer that is brewed and bottled in Germany still states on its label that the company has been in existence since 1383. Some fine German brews still bear the names of the religious orders which first made them.

Long ago (as well as today), people liked their beers in different shades and in different textures. One strange test for beer's quality was the practice of sitting on beer on a leather bench to see if one's leather pants stuck to it when it had evaporated. If the pants did not stick, the beer was considered impure.

Today, the quality of beer is controlled both by very old and by very modern methods. In Pilsen, the beer is still made by the same method that was used hundreds of years ago. The boilers are fired by coal, the fermentation takes place in huge oak casks in tremendous caves beneath the city. The brewing time is still 25 weeks, even though it is only about 3 or 4 weeks in modern breweries. But the real Pilsen beer is considered king of beers.

In contrast to this, modern breweries use electronic techniques and insist on spotless conditions. Yeast may be cultivated in germ-free laboratories, since contamination by other microscopic plants can ruin an entire batch of beer. Much scrubbing and cleaning of equipment and hospital-like cleanliness among workers helps to guarantee uniform quality in the brews.

There are thousands of variations in the process by which beer is made, but all involve some of the basic things. For example, malt is a basic ingredient, and the process of malting is the sprouting of barley grains and other cereals so that the starch in them is converted into sugar, for yeast cannot ferment starch. Then after the grains and other cereals sprout, they are dried by heating to a temperature of about 180°F. The sprout is killed, but a large quantity of the starch-splitting enzyme formed during the sprouting remains, and more starch is rapidly changed to maltose or malt.

Malt is then carefully dried and ground up. This material is mixed with about 3 parts water and boiled. The resulting product is known as mash.

The brewmaster supervises the mixing, the

standing, and the cooking, along with other procedures that are necessary for the proper quality of the finished beer.

The temperature and the length of time at which the mash is maintained at a given temperature determines how much of the substance will be fermentable. The part which does not ferment gives the "body" to the brew. Today, all these operations are controlled very scientifically so that a uniform product results.

In some cases, the solids are allowed to settle on the bottom of the mixture after stirring and they form a natural filter. The liquid part is called wort, and this passes through the solids into the brewing kettle. The solids are rinsed with water in order to obtain all the flavor, and the rinse water is added to the wort.

Now hops are added to the mixture. Hops are used to give brews bitterness and character. Only the flower or cone from the female hop vine is used. This is like a small pine cone with very soft leaves, and it must be picked at just the right time. The leaves and stems are discarded, and the cone is carefully dried to preserve its fine delicate aroma. The aroma of the hops is very important to the character of the beer.

Hops are stored in clean chambers at a temperature of about 40°F. They are subjected to careful chemical analyses to determine the kinds of resins they contain. Hops not only add flavor to the beer, but they help to prevent the development of wild bacteria which might get into the mixture.

Next the mixture is boiled for several hours. This sterilizes it further, removes excess water, accomplishes the evaporation of some of the bitter flavoring materials from the hops, and makes other insoluble substances dissolve. During this process, there is some caramelization, and the mixture darkens in color.

Perhaps you have wondered why yeast is kept in germ-free laboratories in some breweries. When the beer making reaches the stage described in the paragraph above, it is ready for fermentation. The kind of yeast has much to do with determining the characteristics of the beer. If it is to be uniform, no foreign strains may be present. In addition to the alcohol which forms in the process of fermentation, there are other products of fermentation which influence the character of the beer. The nature of the yeast plants used in the process determines these important characteristics. These substances, other than alcohol and water, are called congeners.

Congeners are responsible for the variations in flavor. As many as 2,000 varieties of beers may be purchased in the pubs of the British Isles. German beer halls offer a wide variety of excellent beers, and one can find as many as 1,400 different breweries in Bavaria alone. No other area has this many. Bavaria is famous for its beautiful landscape and for its beer. Here the famous beer festival, Oktoberfest, attracts millions of people each fall and many kinds of beer are drunk during this 16-day festival.

Beer at festivals and in public places is usually served from the kegs and is called draught beer. When serving beer from bottles and cans, there is an art to pouring it into glasses. First, never use glasses that have been washed in soap, for soapy water may leave a film on the inside of the glass that destroys the carbon dioxide. Pour the beer directly toward the center of the bottom of the glass at a medium, or natural, speed so that a foamy head is formed to protect the carbonation in the beer while it is being drunk.

Bottled beer should be stored in a dark place to prevent change in flavor. Both bottles and cans should be stored in a cool place. When refrigerated, bottles should be kept upright so that the smallest amount of liquid surface is exposed to the small amount of air in the bottle. This helps to keep the beer from going flat.

Beer comes in many shades from "white" to "black," and it is used for many purposes. Russians consider it an antidote to drunkenness. Some Africans wash their babies in it, and many

Americans wash their hair in beer. Nigerian men drink it, hoping to increase their virility. African Bantu tribes prize beer for the food value and are careful to preserve the minerals, vitamins, and other nutrients. Most people drink it because they enjoy the taste, its thirst-quenching, and its relaxing qualities.

Wine

Properly speaking, wine is the fermented juice of grapes. The word wine is often used for fermented drinks which are made from various fruits and vegetables, but, when these are made, sugar must be added. Not enough sugar is present naturally to make them palatable. Today, hard apple cider is sometimes called apple wine. Perry from pears, elderberry, blackberry, and dandelion are just a few "wines" not made from grapes. In some countries, beer is referred to as barley wine. But the true wine comes from grapes.

Beverage wines, wines which are drunk with meals, contain between 7 and 14% alcohol. Some popular wines in this group are Claret, Moselle, Burgundy, Sauternes, and Hock. They are generally classed as red or white. Those which contain just the slightest tinge of red may be referred to as rosé and appear pink, but they are usually classed as red wine.

The color of wine is determined by the color of the grapes from which the wine is made. Red wine comes from dark grapes, and white wines are made from either black or white grapes. If black grapes are used, the skins are separated from them before fermentation takes place and the coloring does not get into the wine. The juice from most varieties of black grapes is colorless. The white wines are not really white, but vary from a pale, straw color to a deep, dark brown. No wines are really colorless.

Wines which are usually drunk before or after meals are those which contain a higher percentage of alcohol and are known as fortified wines. Many have an alcoholic strength of 18 to 20%, or possibly more. These include Sherry, Madeira, and Port. In order to fortify, or increase, the amount of alcohol in the wine, alcohol is added at the end of the fermentation process. Fermentation stops naturally when it reaches the point where the yeast can no longer live in a greater concentration of alcohol. For certain wines, the alcohol is added when the fermentation has not been completed, and some sugar is left unfermented. Such wine is very sweet.

Sparkling wine is a special variety in which a second fermentation is carried on after the wine is bottled. In the case of top quality sparkling wines, this is done by adding extra sugar and yeast. Less expensive sparkling wines are prepared by cooling a wine and forcing carbon dioxide into them. Sparkling wines include Asti Spumante, sparkling Moselle, sparkling Burgundy, and the "king of wines," champagne.

In addition to beverage, fortified, and sparkling wines, there is a fourth group known as Vermouth. Vermouth comes in two types: Italian and French. The Italian is sweet and the French is dry, although not as dry as ordinary beverage wine. Vermouth differs from other wines through the addition of herbs, one of which is wormwood, a bitter, aromatic herb. There may be as many as 40 or 50 herbs in a vermouth. The wine base of the Vermouth differs according to whether or not sweet or dry Vermouth is being produced. In either case, it is a fortified wine which contains 15% or more alcohol.

The beverage wines, or those which contain less than 15% alcoholic content, improve with age after bottling. With the exception of vintage ports, other wines improve very little or do not improve at all after bottling.

Wine has increased in popularity within the past few years at a pace known by no other beverage. Americans have often been called coffee-drinking, water-drinking, rum-drinking, and whisky-drinking people. Today, some young adults consider themselves as a group of wine drinkers. The average American adult still drinks considerably less wine than most Europeans, but the wine industry in the United States is growing rapidly and American wines are increasing in quality. Some are being exported to countries that are famous for their own good wines.

What makes a good wine? The answer to this question depends somewhat on the individual's taste, but there are certain general qualities which wine experts, or oenologists, consider in comparing wines. They look for characteristics such as color, taste, and aroma. While certain wines are considered suitable for special uses, there is always a long way from a poor wine to an excellent one. What makes this difference?

One of the factors which determines the quality of a wine is the land that produces the grapes. The chemical composition of the product is determined partly by the soil in which the grapevines are grown. One might expect excellent wines to come from grapes that grow in excellent soils, but such is not necessarily the case. For example, the Bordeaux district of France, which has been famous for its wines for more than 2,000 years, has mainly gravel, limestone, and sand as the soil in which its grapes grow. Certainly, this is far from what one usually considers as rich soil, but it is the kind of soil in which vines bear excellent quality grapes for some of the finest wines in the world. Many famous regions in Europe grow their grapes in soil that would not be good for vegetable growing or other agriculture uses.

The geography of the countryside is so important in determining the quality of wine that many wines have been named for the regions in which they grow. Just the right combinations of soil, the right temperatures at the right times, sunshine, moisture, and the angle of the slope on which the vines grow help to determine the quality of the grapes.

Warm springs play an important part in producing the flowers of the grapevine. These set the grapes that then fill to maturity. The good years and the bad years vary because of the weather. In Western Europe, where some of the best grapes grow, cold and rainy summers or very hot ones are less than welcome by the grape growers for such summers produce grapes that give poor, acid wine. The chemical content of the grape, which in turn determines the chemical content, the taste, and aroma of the wine, is dependent a great deal upon the slow ripening of grapes in most favorable conditions of sun, rain, and temperature. Picture two vineyards that are separated by hills. For one, the year may be a good one, but the rain may have been stopped by the hill so the vineyard on the other side might have had a dry spring, a dry summer, and a poor year. While the tables which tell of the good and bad years of the various wine districts of Europe are generally reliable, there may be many variations. Even vine-tending, blending, and handling play a part in the quality of the final product.

The grapes themselves which are used for wine-making come from a single species known as *Vitis vinifera.* These grapes differ considerably from the vast varieties of wild grapes which are found in many parts of the world where grapes can grow. There are even numerous varieties of Vitis vinifera. Perhaps as many as 100 different kinds of grapes are used in France alone. Just transplanting a vine from one region to another can change its characteristics over a period of time.

The three most famous wine grapes are the Riesling, the Cabernet-Sauvignon, and the Pinot Noir, but the varieties which make excellent wines form a long long list.

Cultivating the vine so that the grape will be at its best is an art indeed. Caring for the grape-vine so that it is free of diseases and pests is just one phase of this art that has been developed through the centuries. Even the exact time at which the grape should be picked is a very important factor in obtaining the best flavor.

Much care is taken in harvesting the grapes. Sometimes grapes are snipped individually with tiny scissors. Various treatment of the stems, the pips, and the skins play a part in the taste of the wine. Grapes are separated from the stems, and the juice is freed from the grapes by modern and by the very old ways including, in some cases, the treading which is so famous. The combination of skins, pips, and juice is fermented according to the custom of the vinter. And so it is that the natural course of fermentation is modified to produce the best-tasting wine.

A number of kinds of yeast, including the important one which is known as saccharomycetes, appear on the skin of the grapes when they begin to ripen. But the yeast can begin the process of fermentation only after the grapes are gathered and crushed. Some of the wild yeasts die when the alcohol level reaches 4%, but the true wine yeasts, the saccharomycetes, take control and raise the alcohol content to a greater degree. If there is enough sugar in the grapes, the content may reach 12 to 14% before all the yeast plants die.

Suppose you could look into a vat of must, or new wine. There you would see what appears to be a bubbling, or boiling, liquid. The skins, pips, and other parts of the vine float to the top where they form a layer that may be as great as 4 feet thick. The must which is beneath it slowly becomes wine. At this point, between a week and a month after the fermentation began, the new wine is drawn off into clean casks and placed in the cellar or warehouse. Fermentation continues slowly after this. A water seal is used so that the gas which it forms may continue to escape without allowing air to enter the cask.

There is some loss of wine during the first few months, so new wine is added to prevent spoiling, or the turning of wine to vinegar. Casks are refilled twice a week during the first few months and biweekly until about 6 months has passed and the wine has become clear.

As the wine is changing, some impurities fall to the bottom of the cask. These are known as lees. If the lees remain in contact with the good wine for too long, they interfere with its quality. In order to prevent this, wine is moved into different casks several times during its first year. Even in this process, the weather must be considered. The operation must take place on a clear, dry day. It it does not, the wine may become dull in appearance.

By the time the wine is put into the third cask, the containers are laid on their sides, and the only air which can come in contact with the wine is through the porous wood.

Wine remains in the wooden casks for several years, depending on quality and type of wine. When it is bottled, once more a clear day is chosen. It has been said that wine is a living thing. In the wine trade, there is an expression known as bottle sickness. This is due to the fact that the changing of the wine from the cask to the bottle interferes with its progress. Wine that has been freshly bottled is not drinkable. The wine adjusts to its new environment after a while and continues its fermentation in a normal manner. Wine that remains in the bottle too long is said to be dead. This means that the wine has lost its flavor, its body, its aroma, and its color.

Just as no two people are alike, no two wines are alike. Wines are said to have their own personalities, and the words used in describing wines have special meanings. Dry is the opposite of sweet. Acidity gives bite to the flavor and is an important quality which adds to the aroma. Experts speak of the character of the wine. They describe wine in terms such as depth, which is a subtle richness that gives the feeling of many flavor layers. A wine may be foxy, meaning it has a spicy tang. It might be light, or full-bodied, in connection with the tactile sense that it imparts to the tongue. A ripe wine is mellow and has reached its full bloom of maturity. A rich wine has a good combination of fruit flavor and body. A velvety wine has a special, silky smoothness, while a delicate wine is a light one with an agreeable flavor and quality. A big wine is one that is strong in flavor and high in alcohol content. Woody wines have a particular odor from aging in oak casks. Fruity wines are those which are just pleasantly ripe. Deep wines are those that are full and rich in bouquet.

White wines are always delicate wines and many people prefer them to the red wines. Red wines are favorites of most Americans who like their body and color. But both red and white come in numerous varieties of taste, aroma, and color.

Storing of wines is important only in the case of those which continue to age. Such wines should be stored by laying the bottle on its side. If you do not own a storage rack, one can be made from a carton with compartments; from wooden boxes; wooden squares set on a diagonal; or clay pipes. A cool, quiet place is best.

Wine can be drunk from a glass of any quality shape or size, but there is an advantage in having a glass that is smaller at the lip than in the middle in that it intensifies the bouquet and helps the drinker to enjoy the aroma and the taste of the wine volatiles, the properties which are released when the wine evaporates. Wine glasses are usually filled just halfway and should be large enough to hold about 3 or 4 ounces without the wine reaching the top of the glass.

Many experts have developed a process known as "whistling in." They take about half a teaspoon of wine in the mouth, then suck in air to cause the alcohol to evaporate. This helps them to explore the qualities of the wine as it is swirled around in the mouth and brought into touch with the taste buds.

Many people prefer to drink white and pink wines at a temperature of about 50° F and red wines at a temperature of about 60° F. Old wines, and those of outstanding quality, are best served at room temperature. Placing a bottle of wine on the bottom shelf of the refrigerator for about an hour usually brings it to a temperature that is best for drinking, but sudden chilling in the freezer may tend to hurt the wine.

The cork should be removed slowly, and the

bottle turned slowly as it is lifted from the glass so that the wine does not drip out. A bottle of wine should be opened about a half hour before the time it is served for the best taste results.

The host of today tastes the wine first for a reason different from that used in ancient times. It was traditional for noblemen to use professional wine tasters or to taste the wine themselves before serving the wine to guests to be certain of its quality. Today, the host takes the first glass just in case cork particles may have fallen into it.

Whether you drink wine before a meal, during a meal, or after a meal depends upon your individual taste and upon the kind of wine you choose. Although wine is relatively low in alcohol content, people who drink too much wine too often can become dependent on the alcohol in wine. Such alcoholics are nicknamed "winos." Since the greatest amount of alcohol for the least amount of money can be obtained through inexpensive fortified wines, one often finds the poor alcoholic getting his alcohol supply through the drinking of wine.

To most people, wine is of value because it adds to the enjoyment of a meal. In some cases, wine is of value because it provides needed calories to those who have trouble because of poor appetite. Sometimes, doctors prescribe wine before bedtime to help patients sleep. Even though doctors disagree on the value of wine in improving appetite and in its use as a sedative, few argue about its ability to improve morale. Some even consider small amounts of alcohol, as found in limited amounts of wine, to be one of the world's best antidotes for stress. Certainly, wine is the world's oldest tranquilizer. Just as with any medication, there is a large difference between use and abuse.

The use of wine in religious rituals continues today on a large scale. (Dionysus and Bacchus became the most popular god among the Greeks and the Romans.) And for many modern religious ceremonies, wine plays a major role. Even for the nonreligious, wine plays a significant part in rites of passage through life: at births, initiations, marriages, and funerals.

More and more people are learning to appreciate good quality wine. To explore different wines, educating one's palate to distinguish poor wines from excellent, is a pleasant form of learning.

Distilled
Spirits

While wine is primarily a mealtime beverage, distilled spirits, or liquors, are called the "social lubricant." Since distilled spirits have a higher alcohol content, the feeling of relaxation and other effects on the body happen faster.

The alcoholic content of various beverages varies greatly, and is, in a way, confusing. Beer alcohol is measured in terms of weight, while alcohol content in wine and liquor is stated in terms of volume. Beer which has 3.2% alcohol by weight is the equivalent of 4.0% alcohol by volume. The conversion factor of 0.8 helps in comparing the true amount of alcohol in beer with that of wine and liquor. For example, if you wanted to know the amount by weight of some wine, you could multiply the alcohol content by 0.8.

Proof is another confusing measure of alcohol. In the United States, 100 proof means 50% alcohol by volume. Bourbon marked "Bottled in Bond" is legally 100 proof, or 50% alcohol. Vodkas may come in this same strength or less. On the whole, whiskeys are 86 proof. Gins vary from 80 to 94 proof and rum and brandy are usually 80 proof. There is one brand of rum which is the most potent liquor in the American proof system. This is the kind used in hot buttered rum, and is usually 150 proof.

All of the above alcoholic beverages are made in different ways and are classed according to certain qualifications. Whole books could be written about each type of beverage. Briefly, here is some information that will acquaint you with the characteristics of the most popular kinds.

WHISKEY

In America, whiskey can be classified in three ways: straight, blended straight, or blended. Both rye and bourbon fall in the category of straight whiskey, and only straight whiskeys can be Bottled in Bond. This term applies to whiskey that has been bottled at 100 proof and kept in a bonded warehouse for at least 4 years. The distiller need not pay a tax at the time of bottling, but must do so when he is ready to sell. Bottled in Bond is concerned with a tax arrangement and is no guarantee of the purity or quality of a beverage.

In the case of straight whiskey, the predominant grain which is used for fermentation and distillation determines the label. For example, if more of the grain is corn than rye, the whiskey will be labeled straight bourbon. If more than 51% is wheat, it will be labeled straight wheat whiskey. If more than half is rye, it will be straight rye, and so on. Malt is mixed with various grains to convert the starch in them into the form from which yeast can make alcohol.

Probably about half of the whiskey produced in the United States is blended whiskey. Blending is a science and an art of carefully mixing straight whiskeys with neutral spirits so as to produce a uniform and desirable product. Neutral spirits are almost pure alcohol, obtained by distilling the original grain to 190 proof or higher. At this point, almost all flavor from the original material has been lost.

In some large Eastern cities in the United States, there is confusion between blended whiskey and rye, and those who want a blended whiskey often order rye. Actually, any combinations of grains may be used to produce a true blended whiskey.

Canadian whiskey is a distinctive type which must comply with the laws of Canada. It may contain no distilled spirits less than 2 years old, must be manufactured in Canada, and may not be a straight whiskey. Canadian whiskey must be produced from a cereal grain, but rye is not the only one that may be used. Corn, wheat, and barley are other sources. Grains are used in exact proportions to the formula of the individual distiller.

Scotch whiskey has a smoky flavor because the malt from which it is made is dried over a peat fire. It is produced in Scotland with a primary base of barley for the heavy-bodied type and corn for the lighter-bodied type. Scotch is aged for at least 3 years in uncharred oak barrels or used sherry casks. Generally, it is allowed to remain in the barrels or casks for 5 or more years before bottling.

There are other whiskeys such as Scotch type which is composed of a blend. Sour mash whiskey is a type produced by using part of the previous day's mash instead of water to start the fermentation of the new batch of mash. Irish whiskey is a distinctive product of Northern Ireland that is made from barley.

GIN

Gin is made from a base of neutral spirits which may be produced from grain or molasses, or from the redistillation of any other beverage. The spirits lack a distinctive taste, color, or odor. To give gin its characteristics, herbs and other plant materials are added. Juniper berries, cassia bark, orange peel, caraway, orris root, lemon, anise, and cocoa may be used in various combinations. The exact formula of each distiller's gin is a secret. Ways of distilling gin vary, too. Sometimes, the herbs and other plants are mixed with the neutral spirits and the entire mash is distilled. Sometimes wire mesh traps are used to suspend the herbs above the spirit in the still.

As the vapors rise, they pass through and around these materials and are impregnated with the flavoring oils that are contained in them.

The vapors which are recovered from the gin still are 100 to 180 proof. They are reduced to bottling strength, which is between 80 and 94 proof, before they are marketed.

True gin falls into two classes: Dutch and dry. The Dutch is full-bodied and possesses a malty odor and taste. Dry gin is English or American gin and is lighter in flavor and body with more of a fragrant aroma and taste.

Gin does· not require aging, although some distillers do age their gin for periods of time in wood. This give the gin a light golden color. Whether dry or Dutch gin, the beverage is ready for drinking as it comes from the still.

Gin is used in combinations in many popular drinks, and is sometimes drunk straight. The latter is especially true of Holland gin.

VODKA

Vodka is another alcoholic beverage which is not aged, but unlike gin, it is not flavored. Many people think that all vodka is made from potatoes, but this is far from the case. The distiller uses whatever starchy material, potato or grain, which is most readily available to him. By definition, vodka is neutral spirits distilled from any starchy material above 190 proof, bottled between 80 and 110 proof, and without distinctive character, aroma, and taste.

While gin was originally produced in Holland, vodka originally came from Russia. Today both are made in large quantities in many countries around the world.

RUM

Rum is an alcoholic beverage distilled from the fermented juice of sugar cane, sugar cane molasses, sugar cane syrup, or any other sugar cane by-product.

Rum that is made in the West Indies has long been famous, and much of the world's rum is produced on these islands. There are three main kinds of rum: light-bodied, dry rums; full-bodied, rich rums; and aromatic rums which come from Java. Labels on rum bottles show the geographical area in which the rum was produced.

BRANDIES

Brandies are beverages distilled from grapes, apples, peaches, raisins, and other fruits. Cognac is a brandy distilled from grapes grown in a certain area of France, and it takes its name from the city, Cognac. There are many brandies from many countries, and many kinds from each country. Most are sweet after-dinner drinks, but some are popular for use in cooking and combined with coffee. All brandies may be used in making mixed drinks.

CORDIALS AND LIQUEURS

Distilled spirits which contain fruits, juices, herbs, flowers, or other flavorings along with a minimum of 2-1/2% sugar by weight are popular after-dinner drinks. They are numerous, and enjoyed for their flavor more than their alcoholic content which is minimal in effect since only very small amounts are usually sipped slowly.

Two very famous liqueurs were first produced as medicines in monasteries and their exact formulas are still held secret. Benedictine is made from a combination of 27 plants and is made by a process that takes more than 5 years. Although the exact proportions of ingredients is passed down through the years, it is claimed that only three people know the exact formula at any one time. This liqueur is now produced commercially.

Chartreuse is another liqueur that was developed in a monestary as a medicine and whose formula is held secret by the monks. There are two types of chartreuse, a yellow and a green. It is still made by the Carthusian monks, whose order perfected its formula.

The list of popular liqueurs is long and the flavors vary widely.

This is just a brief introduction to the distilled spirits or so-called hard liquors. Individual tastes, personal health, and body chemistry all play a part in how much of any one is a good or bad thing for any person.

In an effort to find out which drinks produced the worst hangovers, a British scientist experimented with a group of men and women at Middlesex Hospital in England. Those who drank gin, vodka, or white wine suffered less than those who drank rum, whiskey, or brandy. This lends support, according to Dr. Gaston Pavon who directed the experiment, to the theory that certain compounds present in the drinks play a part in producing hangovers. These compounds, known as congeners, are natural products, but they are more common in some beverages than others. Not all are toxic. Some, such as salts, amino acids, vitamins, and sugar have some nutritional value. Others, such as tannins, aldehydes, fusel oil, furfural, and esters are chemicals that seem to upset the body chemistry so that nausea and headaches result if there is too much intake. Some other research on the cause of hangovers is discussed in a later chapter.

Although not everyone agrees on the amount which congeners play in a "recipe for a hangover," they do add to the problems caused by too much alcohol. Here is a way of comparing the amount of congeners: In each 2 ounces of vodka, there is 1.3 milligrams of congeners; in the same amount of Scotch, there is 40 milligrams; in blended bourbon, 50 milligrams; in cognac 100; and in straight bourbon, about 120 milligrams.

How much you drink may be far more important than what you drink. But how much is too much? How much is too much when you drive?

Social Drinking, Problem Drinking, and Driving

The slogan, "If You Drink Don't Drive and If You Drive, Don't Drink," has been heard by many. Unfortunately, slogans are usually heard but not heeded, especially by problem drinkers. Most people who drink also drive but know how to separate the two acts.

Is there a way of knowing when it is safe to drink and drive? How much is safe? What is the difference between the behavior of a social drinker behind the wheel and that of a problem drinker? What can be done to change the statistics that show that more than half the fatal accidents in the United States involve the driver who has a blood alcohol concentration of 0.10% or higher?

Blood alcohol content is measured in a number of ways. Usually, a person's breath is analyzed, but blood alcohol concentration may be determined from urine, saliva, or the blood itself.

Blood alcohol concentration depends on several things. They include one's body weight, the amount of alcohol consumed (the number and strength of drinks), the time elapsed since drinking began and ended, the amount and kind of food in the stomach at the time of drinking, fatigue, and other factors.

According to the legal standards in most states, it is not considered unsafe to drive with a blood alcohol concentration of less than 0.05%, but with blood alcohol concentrations from 0.05% to 0.10%, it is considered admissible evidence for court in cases of crash involvement. All drivers are presumed impaired at blood alcohol concentrations of 0.10% or greater.

Laws may be guidelines, but no two people react to alcohol the same way nor does an individual person necessarily react to alcohol the same way at different times. Even one's mood can affect the results to some degree. Driving *experience* is another factor involved in the safety, or danger, of driving after drinking more than a single ounce. If you decide to drink and need to drive afterward, arrange for an alternate driver or a ride home in another car in advance. A decision to drive after drinking that is made *after* one has started drinking is frequently a poor one because of the alcoholic euphoria which leads one to believe that he can do anything in the world better than anyone else.

One rule to follow is to wait at least 1 hour per average drink before driving. This is the minimum amount of time that your body needs to rid itself of alcohol it has absorbed.

In considering when it is safe to drive, one must consider the use and effect of any other drugs as well as the effect of the alcohol since studies have shown that alcohol and certain other drugs taken in combination have a synergistic effect. This means that the two produce an effect greater than the sum of the two individual drugs if taken separately, from the standpoint of impaired ability. For example, suppose you have taken some antihistamine during the day because you have a cold. You have a drink before dinner, and then you drive. Your ability is impaired to a greater extent by the combination of these two drugs than it would be if they did not react so that two plus two has the same effect as six rather than four. Alcohol plays a major role in a very large percentage of accidents; no one knows exactly how many, but half the fatalities are attributed to drinking drivers.

The National Highway Traffic Safety Administration of the Department of Transportation of the United States, The National Safety Council, The National Institute on Alcohol Abuse and Alcoholism, and many other groups are doing research and putting programs in operation that will help to remove the drunken driver from the road. The expertise of psychologists, psychiatrists, highway engineers, automotive engineers, toxicologists, attornies, policemen, and others are being combined to learn more about the problem of drinking and driving for users and abusers of alcohol. They define the social drinker as one who is a law-abiding citizen and a responsible person. Sometimes, the social drinker does become intoxicated, and sometimes, the social drinker does drive. The problem drinker-driver is defined as a person who either has a very high blood alcohol concentration (in excess of 0.25%) at the time of some incident or who has one or more arrests for other offenses involving alcohol, including non-highway arrests. Problem drinkers are frequently known to various health and social agencies in the community and often have a history of troubled relationships with employers, family, and friends because of their drinking.

As long ago as 1968, *The Alcohol and Highway Safety Report* recognized that alcoholics and other problem drinkers account for a very large part of the overall problem of alcohol-related accidents, and this is still true today. Even though they account for only about seven percent of the drivers in the United States, the problem drinker-drivers are responsible for two out of three alcohol-related deaths that occur on the highways of the United States.

Problem drinkers do not respond to penalties, no matter how harsh. For example, the Department of Transportation estimates that 80 percent of the drivers whose licenses have been suspended or revoked for repeated drunken driving offenses continue to drive anyway.

As a result of studies in highway safety and the Federal Motor Vehicle and Safety Act of 1966, money was made available for research projects aimed to keep the problem drinker off the highway. One of these was Project ABETS (*A*spects, *B*ehavioral and *E*nvironmental in *T*raffic *S*afety), which consists of an interdisciplinary team of scientists (psychologists, statisticians, epidemiologists, pathologists, and so forth) at the University of Vermont. Since the formation of Project ABETS in 1967, this team has conducted many interesting studies and experiments that have been carried out in their laboratories, in the field, and under actual driving conditions on closed courses. For example, many volunteer subjects took part in one group of the experiments in which a special automobile is used, one known as a "Highway Systems Research" car. This is actually an electro-mechanical laboratory on wheels which was originally developed, in part, by the Ford Motor Company. There are two control consoles of lights and counting devices, one mounted under the dashboard and one on the driveshaft hump. Basically, the automobile is like any other, but it contains about $30,000 worth of sophisticated electronic and mechanical equipment. This makes it possible for psychologists, who are studying driving behavior, to measure and record performance at the wheel. They can measure and record psychological and physiological stress experienced by the driver when he passes another car, turns, merges with traffic, or meets other situations on the highway.

Suppose you are taking part in an experiment in which you will be driving at 40 miles per hour on a controlled course when you are drunk. You have already been given a battery of psychological tests so that much is known about your personality. You are prepared on the day of the test by drinking an exact amount of alcohol, based on your weight, so that your blood alcohol level will be 0.10%. For a 150-pound person, on an empty stomach, this is the equivalent of five beers per hour. You get legally drunk. In this particular experiment, you will be driving on a deserted drag strip where there are some obstacles along the course. Sensors and counting devices will record your use of the steering wheel, brakes, and the accelerator. Instruments will check and record periods of time during which you drive with one hand, your mileage, your speed, and the changes of your speed. At the same time, equipment will record your heartbeat and your galvanic skin response. The latter is a measure of stress based upon perspiration, since people perspire under stress. Your steering wheel, which is gold-plated, is an excellent conductor of electrical impulses and these records can be made without electrodes being attached to your body.

When you have finished the experiment, the information which has been gathered about your driving behavior will be studied in minute detail as part of Project ABETS research program. The driving task, which has been administered to 150 volunteers, is only one part of many complex studies being conducted in Project ABETS on the effects of alcohol upon selected aspects of driving.

Among the many conclusions drawn from studies of drivers in the experimental car were the following (when doses of alcohol large enough were given to bring blood alcohol content to the level in which a driver is considered legally impaired): 1) reduced performance on both visual auditory attention tasks which require the monitoring of multichannel inputs; 2) decreased responsiveness to stimulation of the eye when source comes from sides, resulting in a type of "tunnel vision"; 3) alteration of what driver sees or thinks he sees in ambiguous situations; 4) increases in the likelihood of risky behavior in chance-taking situations; 5) different mood or performance effects with respect to personality characteristics; and 6) reductions in driving accuracy and changes in control-use patterns.

In another aspect of the experimental program, you may go to a class in which one half of the students who have volunteered are given a very small amount of alcoholic beverage and the other half have been given a larger amount. Both amounts are based on a computer print-out which will produce a known blood alcohol concentration level for each person, according to individual weight. Then mental tests are administered to determine how well the students can perform: without alcohol, with low dosage, and with high dosage. These results are compared with large numbers of tests to help identify what happens when one drives while intoxicated in the real world.

Dr. M. W. Perrine and his associates at Project ABETS made many recommendations, in their final report of September 1971, concerning individuals who drive while intoxicated, based on definitive observations of what such drivers see, the way they pay attention, the way they identify things, and their emotional influences.

The study confirmed that young male drivers who drink are very high-risk drivers even though their blood alcohol content may be lower than that of an experienced driver. For them, there is the combination of trying to learn to do two things at the same time: learning to drink and to drive. Girls do not drive as often or as much, so the percentage of accident involvement for females in this age group is not as great as for males. The surrender of the car keys to a sober girl after a party might save many lives.

From ABETS came many recommendations relevant to highway safety action programs concerning alcohol, sponsored by the federal government (USDOT). One of these was that the study had convincingly reconfirmed the marked overrepresentation of problem drinkers and other heavy users of alcohol among those responsible for serious and fatal highway crashes and other serious moving violations. It was recommended that the present emphasis of the Department of Transportation upon identification and control of this type of drinker should be continued.

There was a marked overrepresentation of *beer drinkers* among those arrested and among fatalities in alcohol-connected accidents. Among the recommendations is one that films and television spots show scenes in which the drinking of alcoholic beverages leads to difficulty.

Although problem drinkers were markedly overrepresented among those who got into trouble on the highway in this study, there was a substantial proportion of *young social drinkers.* It was recommended that emphasis be given to this fact in countermeasure programs of the Department of Transportation.

Individuals who have a number of arrests for driving while intoxicated were hard to locate. Since they move frequently from one area to another, it was suggested that rehabilitation programs for such individuals establish mechanisms to maintain a close watch on them.

The list of recommendations from these

studies and others is long, but the ABETS results and recommendations played an important part in the development of a new federal program called ASAP (Alcohol Safety Action Projects) in which about 35 community programs are at work identifying problem drinkers and steering them into rehabilitation programs which keep them off the highway, at least until each person's alcohol and driving problem is solved.

Each ASAP program functions in a slightly different way. For example, in New Orleans, there is a permanent van where people who have been drinking may take a breath test to determine if they have a blood alcohol content above the 0.10% level. If they do, they are offered a ride home. In Tampa, Florida, judges are guided by the results of a questionnaire and interview given to offenders to separate social from problem drinkers. A special investigator in Portland, Maine, follows the activities of those who have had licenses suspended or revoked for drunken driving. In some areas, behavior modification programs are used rather than 30 days in jail. Personality tests are given before and after the program in an effort to determine whether or not the individual has been convinced of his problem.

In Los Angeles, where a large program is under way, the drunk driver is classified as a social drinker who did something unusual or as a problem drinker who frequently drives while drunk. Problem drinkers are offered a choice of rehabilitation programs. Some are given disulfiram, a compound that causes a person to vomit if he drinks alcoholic beverages.

The most unique feature of Project CRASH, the Vermont ASAP, is the so-called "Driver Profile." For this countermeasure, a special questionnaire has been developed to aid in identifying the problem-drinking driver on the basis of psychological variables *before* he gets into trouble. The questionnaire is administered by the Department of Motor Vehicles when the person takes his tests for the state driver's license. The rationale for using psychometric methods to improve driver-licensing programs is based on the assumption that individuals who subsequently become labeled as "bad" or high-risk drivers in terms of crashes and violations differ systematically on some combination of biographical, attitudinal, and personality variables which can be measured before the fact; that is, can be obtained when the individual submits himself as an applicant for a driving license. In other words, it is assumed that there are systematic differences between these high-risk drivers and those drivers who can be defined as low risk in terms of a subsequent crash- and citation-free driving record. The studies already conducted at Project ABETS show that this approach has considerable promise, is feasible, and is worth pursuing. It should be noted that, at this time, an individual who shows as a probable high-risk driver is not refused his driver's license, but it is recommended that he take advantage of reeducation, counseling, and even therapy programs which are available.

The local community efforts of today will emphasize coordination with ASAP programs and with all the agencies that may deal with drinker-driving in an effort to keep the problem drinkers off the road. Some cooperating agencies may have little to do with driving but may help to identify problem drinkers, since many have been in trouble at work or in family situations.

Another approach to the problem of drinking and driving is the search for a "sober pill" as described on page 39. Other teams of investigators such as those at Edinburgh University are experimenting with a "sobering up" chemical, using the sugar known as fructose. Some years ago, Harvard Medical School researchers found that blood alcohol levels of alcoholic men were reduced at a rate more rapid than normal by intravenous injections of fructose. In the recent study, in Scotland, the patients who were given the fructose solution sobered up at a rate 25% faster than the controls. But as mentioned earlier, a fructose pill to quickly reduce alcohol level so that it would be safe to drive home from a party has not yet been developed.

Education in when it is safe to drive remains the most important factor in preventing alcohol-related accidents. Knowing how much is safe is an individual matter, but the bar barometer on page 91 is a general guide.

Education in the effect of various beverages on an individual could help, too. Some drinkers are confused by the equivalency of blood alcohol concentration produced by different kinds of alcoholic beverages. In general, 1 ounce of whiskey equals one 12-ounce beer or 4 ounces of table wine. Needless to say, as mentioned earlier, many other factors are involved, but beer is not as innocuous as often considered. It is the implicated beverage in many traffic fatalities where alcohol is involved.

In the 15 to 24 age group, there is a higher probability of dying in a motor accident than from all other ways combined. Far too many traffic deaths, the leading cause of deaths among young people, are alcohol related.

The impact of the drinking and driving problem may be greater if you pick up a newspaper on any day and read about the number of fatal crashes over any weekend. You can bet with confidence that, of the single car fatal crashes, about three fourths of the drivers under 25 years

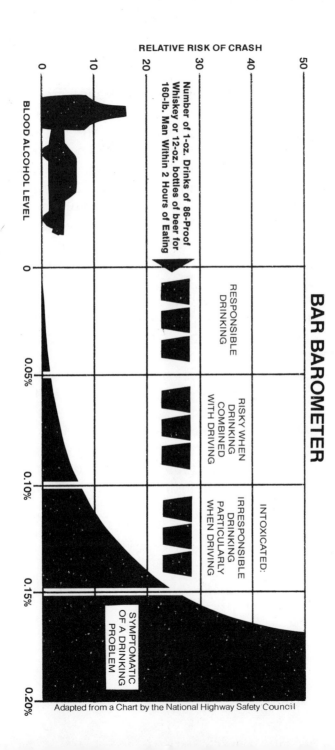

BAR BAROMETER

RELATIVE RISK OF CRASH

50
40
30
20
10
0

Number of 1-oz. Drinks of 86-Proof
Whiskey or 12-oz. bottles of beer for
160-lb. Man Within 2 Hours of Eating

BLOOD ALCOHOL LEVEL

0   0.05%   0.10%   0.15%   0.20%

RESPONSIBLE DRINKING

RISKY WHEN DRINKING COMBINED WITH DRIVING

IRRESPONSIBLE DRINKING PARTICULARLY WHEN DRIVING

INTOXICATED:

SYMPTOMATIC OF A DRINKING PROBLEM

Adapted from a Chart by the National Highway Safety Council

of age had a blood alcohol concentration greater than the legal level.

Many programs of highway safety are attempting to find a positive way of providing understanding, especially for the young people who are just entering the driving society. The punitive approach and the slogans that have been used in the past have been of little value in the alcohol problem. The need for education of the public in general and rehabilitation of the problem drinker are clear. These and other positive countermeasures may help to make the wish to reduce the number of alcohol-related highway accidents a reality.

Most young people who drink do so in a responsible manner. The same is true of their driving. Perhaps the most important countermeasure of all is the peer pressure being brought to bear on the intoxicated drinkers of all age groups by the young people who are aware of the tremendous pile-up of dead and injured caused by their driving.

Do You Know an Alcoholic?

Tom's father is one of the 100,000 new alcoholics which increase the epidemic in the United States each year. The consumption of alcohol is increasing at a rate more than twice as great as the population according to a recent report by the American Hospital Association. Many intelligent people are becoming more and more concerned about the difference between responsible drinking and alcoholism. For Tom's father, the concern is a very personal one. The same is true for Tom and other members of his family, for alcoholism spreads tragedy to more than the individual who is an alcoholic.

Mary's father is a heavy drinker, too. How does he differ from Tom's father? Although not everyone agrees on the definition of an alcoholic, some experts differentiate between the alcoholic's compulsion which makes drinking interfere with some phase of his life and a heavy drinker's ability to control his intake. A social drinker has control, may drink heavily only at times, and probably considers drinking as a pleasurable event rather than a means of coping with problems.

Consider the variations in the definitions of heavy drinkers. Certainly, heavy drinking can mean different things to different people. By one definition, it applies to anyone who drinks nearly every day and has at least five drinks on one occasion per week. In one recent medical book, a heavy drinker is described as one who consumes a pint or more of whiskey a day.

Whenever a person becomes drunk, alcohol abuse is present. When repeated abuse causes problems with an individual's family life, business, social, community life, or interferes with safe driving, alcoholism may be developing.

In true alcoholism, there is a change in the human body so that a person needs increased doses to obtain the same effect. This dependence on alcohol as a drug may be an important way of reacting to problems, may be due to some complex combination of a person's biological and psychological make-up, or may be due to external factors; no matter what the cause, an alcoholic has a problem which progresses. It deteriorates his or her functioning as a responsible person even though his or her life style and value system may be one which the person hates. But the alcoholic usually cannot stop without help from others. Knowing how to help is very important. Many well-meaning people, family included, do more harm than good.

How can one identify the clues which help a drinker to recognize that he has a problem? The National Institute of Alcohol Abuse and Alcoholism of the United States Department of Health, Education and Welfare suggests the following quiz:

1. Do you think and talk about drinking often?
2. Do you drink more now than you used to?

3. Do you sometimes gulp drinks?
4. Do you often take a drink to help you relax?
5. Do you drink when you are alone?
6. Do you sometimes forget what happened while you were drinking?
7. Do you keep a bottle hidden somewhere —at home or at work—for quick pick-me-ups?
8. Do you need a drink to have fun?
9. Do you ever just start drinking without really thinking about it?
10. Do you drink in the morning to relieve a hangover?

If a person answers "yes" to four or more of these ten questions, a drinking problem may exist. Certainly the warning flags are up, and professional help may be needed. Only a doctor can truly diagnose an alcoholic, but even they have difficulty. According to the National Council on Alcoholism, only one doctor in 300 is capable of an accurate diagnosis of alcoholism. If this is the case, you can see that a layman has little basis on which to label a person as an alcoholic.

Recently, criteria to help in the diagnosis of alcoholics were published in two leading medical journals, *the American Journal of Psychiatry* and *the Annals of Internal Medicine.* They describe major symptoms which include: the daily consumptions of a fifth of whiskey or an equivalent amount of beer or wine; failure to appear intoxicated even when alcohol blood level is high; and continued drinking even though there are strong reasons to stop, such as medical, social, job, and/or family problems. Frequent automobile accidents, repeated attempts to stop drinking, secret drinking, outbursts of rage while intoxicated are among symptoms that are listed by these two journals. While these lists are mainly a guide for medical doctors, they help to promote understanding of the disease among the public in general.

Although alcoholics differ from each other, many follow a typical pattern. For example, Jane is a young woman who seemed to enjoy drinking more than most people. In recent years, the amount and frequency of her alcohol intake has increased, but she becomes annoyed if anyone suggests that she really is drinking more than in the past. She avoids some of the concern of her family and friends by drinking secretly. She finds excuses for more social drinking, too, thus easing her own guilt about the amount and frequency. One rule has kept Jane from believing she is an alcoholic. Jane never drinks until after 3 o'clock in the afternoon. Jane has noticed the "blackouts" or temporary loss of memory about what happened when she had been drinking too much. This has made her anxious, but she has always heard that true alcoholics drink in the morning and she never does. How sad that physical damage to her body is the first thing to convince her that her "slogan" is wrong.

Alcoholics and potential alcoholics, as well as people who rarely drink, may believe old sayings such as "all alcoholics drink secretly" or "alcoholism is due to an alcoholic personality," or "most alcoholics are Skid Row personalities."

Actually, Skid Row alcoholism accounts for only about three to five percent of the problem. In the world of industry, an estimated ten billion dollars is lost each year in the United States due to alcohol-related problems of approximately 4.5 million workers. Few of the problem drinkers who cause injuries and death to about half a million people each year are of the Skid Row type. The millions of women who drink belong to a wide range of social groups.

Do you know an alcoholic? Those who answer "no" to this question may know alcoholics but not recognize them as such. At least 95% are employed, or employable, and about 70% belong to communities where they perform more or less effectively as teachers, clergymen, bankers, housewives, farmers, salesmen, doctors, and so on.

Recently alcoholism was found to be a major problem among young people even though this disease usually develops over a period of 5 to 7 years.

Public health officials are finding that many young people taste their first alcoholic beverages at the age of 13. Although relatively few will become problem drinkers, a recent study that was made by Dr. Harold W. Demone, Jr., a Harvard psychiatrist, brought to light some frightening information. For example, among 3,500 boys studied in seven Boston-area junior and senior high schools, there was signs of pathological drinking at the rate of 1.3 percent by the age of 14. By the age of 18 years and older, the study showed 7 percent on occasion abusing alcohol. In this study, 85 percent of the boys under 18 years of age were classed as light, moderate, heavy, relief, or pathological drinkers.

While the above study was based on boys, other studies of teen-age drinking indicate that there is little difference between the amount of alcohol used among girls and boys in the teen-age group.

Recent information gathered by public health officials and other researchers shows that many young people are giving up other drugs in favor of alcohol because it is cheaper and easier to get. Frequently, parents are delighted that their children are using alcohol and not "drugs," thus encouraging alcohol use. If one in 14 show signs of problem drinking before graduation from high school, alcoholism prevention falls in the category of epidemic disease prevention.

Suppose you think someone in your family is an alcoholic. If the person will not go to a doctor or a helping agency, what can you do? Hundreds of young people find an organization known as ALATEEN (P. O. Box 182, Madison Square Station, New York, N.Y. 10010) helpful in coping with the problem of having an alcoholic parent. ALATEEN, started in 1957 by a boy in California whose father was an alcoholic, has grown throughout a wide area. It helps young people understand that such a parent is abnormally sensitive to alcohol physically and that an alcoholic is a compulsive drinker. He or she may want to stop, but the drive for more alcohol is so strong that it overpowers feelings about not wanting to hurt family or self. Few alcoholics will admit their problems, especially since many have been taught that drunkenness is a sign of weakness of character. The guilt felt by an alcoholic often leads to more new drinking as a means of escape from these guilt feelings.

What can a person do to help an alcoholic parent? The obvious home treatment methods which seem so right do not help and often hurt. Scolding, persuasion, pleading, tears, and similar tactics make an alcoholic defensive and increase feelings of guilt which the person usually tries to "drown in drink." Hiding the supply from an alcoholic is notably unsuccessful in effecting a change. One cannot reason an alcoholic into a life without the alcohol craved by his or her body.

Actually, there is nothing that you can do *directly* to help an alcoholic, but there are many things which can be done to encourage the parent to want to help himself or herself. For example, if you learn about the disease and understand that it is a disease, you can better treat an alcoholic with respect and love, and refrain from criticism. A change in a family's attitude may help an alcoholic parent want to seek professional help. Alcoholics' problems should not be shielded and hidden. These people must assume responsibility for their own actions to be motivated to treatment.

Suppose your parents fight because one is an alcoholic. Should you take sides? Professionals feel that you should not, since people do and say things under emotional stress that they may not really mean. You have no control over the life of your parents, but your constant love and confidence that alcoholism can be treated can help them. Since alcoholics often show great hostility toward their families even though they love them, it is best to avoid contact with a person who is out of control. Fighting back does not help. Certainly it is hard to believe that an alcoholic did not deliberately get into compulsive drinking habits.

Living with an alcoholic is a very difficult situation. If there is no ALATEEN group in your neighborhood, you can write for free and inexpensive booklets from Alcoholics Anonymous, Al-Anon Family Group Headquarters, Post Office Box 182, Madison Square Station, New York, N.Y. 10010. Al-Anon Family Groups are people who have relations or close friends who are alcoholics.

What can be done generally to help in prevention and treatment of alcoholism will be discussed in later chapters.

Alcoholism and the Human Body

Even though no one knows exactly when one person who drinks heavily becomes an alcoholic, while another, who drinks the same amount, does not, doctors do know some of the problems prolonged heavy drinking creates in the human body. Alcohol is unique as a drug because it has a food value, or calorie content. A man who has a sedentary job can easily get half his calories by drinking alcohol, but these calories are "empty," meaning that alcohol contains little or no protein, vitamins, and lacks some of the other food factors necessary for the healthy functioning of the body.

Nutritional problems are common among those who drink heavily for long periods. This is especially true since more than lack of proper food elements is involved. Food that is consumed is poorly handled by the liver where the metabolism of alcohol is also taking place. In addition to this, there seems to be an action of alcohol on the system by which liver cells secrete fatty cells into the bloodstream. Some of the fatty droplets may accumulate within the liver cells and damage the liver. This direct effect is still being investigated, but there is no question about the resulting disease. A condition known as cirrhosis of the liver, commonly called fatty liver, develops in about 10% of alcoholics. Since chronic drinking can cause a reduction in animal starch (glycogen) in the liver, low blood sugar can be another organic problem.

The immediate effect of alcohol in the brain from intoxication has been discussed in Chapter 3, but long-term usage has a far different effect. Sustained exposure of central nervous tissue, and especially of brain cells, to alcohol can cause scattered areas of degeneration which gives rise to defects in thinking, memory loss, and personality changes.

Prolonged and heavy use of alcohol can damage the digestive system, since alcohol irritates the stomach and intestines. Constant inflammation may lead to ulceration and internal bleeding. Degenerative changes in the heart muscles of heavy drinkers have been observed, and there are various other problems such as those with kidneys and lungs, that are caused by too much alcohol. Handicaps vary in degree; some heavy drinkers show little organic impairment.

While moderate amounts of alcohol do not usually cause harm in healthy individuals, so many different organs are frequently affected by long-term alcohol abuse that one might wonder why so many people continue to drink too much too often.

For many heavy drinkers, increasing amounts of alcohol are needed to produce euphoria or pleasant feelings. While the majority of social drinkers show little tendency to increase the amounts which they drink, those who depend frequently on a "drug high," or escape route through alcohol, tend to develop an adaptation to it and must increase the dose. After a time, the brain cells require the presence of alcohol in order to function normally. This is known as physiological addiction.

Learning to function under the influence of alcohol enables some alcoholics to appear sober even when they have drunk fairly large amounts. On the other hand, a number of alcoholics develop a sensitivity to the drug, and as little as a single drink produces symptoms of drunkenness in them. This is called reverse tolerance.

True physical dependence to alcohol does not develop as fast, or to the same degree, as addiction to opiates such as heroin, methadone, opium, or other narcotics. Some heavy drinkers never become dependent, but most do after a period of time which varies from 3 to 15 years. This is one reason that authorities are surprised to find so many teen-age alcoholics.

True addiction is a subject of much controversy, but alcohol seems to qualify in the case of some alcoholics. Joel Fort, in his book, *Alcohol: Our Biggest Drug Problem,* states that alcohol addiction is the most serious of any form of addiction, but he does not believe that all alcoholics are addicted to the drug.

Dependency on alcohol is a more gradual

process than dependency on most other drugs, but what happens when a person who is addicted to alcohol stops his drug use can be far more serious than what happens when a heroin addict is deprived of heroin.

When a person who is addicted to alcohol stops drinking abruptly, withdrawal symptoms appear. Some people suffer a mild degree of withdrawal which includes nausea and tremors after only a few days of drinking and after a relatively short period of abstinence. Any alcoholic may show various combinations of withdrawal symptoms, such as nausea, hallucinations, tremors, or convulsive siezures. Shaking may be so severe that a person cannot lift a glass to his or her lips.

Delirium tremens, the most severe form of withdrawal, occurs only in alcoholics who have been drinking over a period of months or even years. The "D.T.'s," as this condition is commonly called, occurs after several days of abstinence. Death occurs in about ten percent of the cases. Artificial respiration, intravenous fluids, and stimulants may be needed. Obviously, hospitalization is necessary in acute cases of withdrawal. Although the patient may seem to recover from physical dependence in about a week, and may recover completely in a month, the psychological dependence remains.

Why do alcoholics who are free of physical

dependence continue to drink when no psychological help follows? A drinker who finds courage, comfort, or a hiding place in a bottle, orients his life around alcohol. He or she drinks compulsively. Such a person lives to drink and physical dependence develops again. Alcoholism has been described as a merry-go-round in which the acute effects become chronic and irreversible.

Alcoholism has been classified in many ways and its causes probed from many angles, but despite thousands of research projects, little is known about the true nature of the disease. A few researchers claim that alcoholism is a bad habit, but most consider it a disease. Some believe it is an allergy. Some claim that alcohol is not the cause of the problem, but people cause it. Certainly, most social drinkers do not become alcoholics.

Most experts agree that alcoholism is an individual problem; there is no such thing as "the alcoholic." Even young people who are just starting to drink vary in their tolerance to alcohol. This is not surprising, since each person has a different body chemistry.

Is there an alcoholic personality? According to some authorities, people who are prone to alcoholism have emotional disturbances which make them unable or unwilling to tolerate large amounts of responsibility, stress, or tension.

They drink to relieve unpleasant feelings of depression, inferiority, anxiety, guilt, hostility, and so on. Each session of coping with problems by drinking tends to establish a pattern of behavior which continues until the condition known as alcoholism is reached and there is physical dependency of their drug of choice. But many authorities believe there is no "alcoholic personality."

A number of alcoholics are believed to be following a path of self destruction and are literally drinking themselves to death in a form of "slow suicide."

What of the people who find themselves in numerous social situations where drinking is custom? And what about heavy drinking as a status symbol? Can these situations lead to alcoholism even if a personality problem does not exist? Since most alcoholics have no obvious psychiatric illness that precedes their addiction to alcohol, this certainly seems a possible factor.

Genetic predisposition may have something to do with the ability of certain people to drink more than others without feeling the effects of the alcohol. Some may inherit an enzyme system which can cope better with alcohol than others in breaking down the poison, or drug, more efficiently. Interesting research is being carried out on genetic predisposition. As to the part genes play in the cause of alcoholism, the question is still being researched (as discussed later).

Perhaps alcohol has a different effect on the brain of a potential alcoholic. Certainly, the way individuals' bodies react to alcohol plays a part in their enjoyment of drinking and in the amount that they drink. For example, some people could never become alcoholics because they are nauseated when they drink small amounts. Others suffer from vertigo, a condition in which a person or his surroundings seem to be whirling about. Some individuals do not like the high feeling which drinking gives them. Others feel it does not do anything for them psychologically; some consider drinking not worth the risk to their health. But for a small minority, alcohol has a special appeal that, for a *complex variety of reasons,* leads them to drinking to the point of addiction and self-destruction. What can be done to help those who are suffering from the physical and other damage which comes with alcoholism is the concern of doctors and paramedics who treat alcoholics and do research in this field. Prevention of alcoholism is the concern of everyone, young and old.

The Puzzle
of Alcoholism

Clues to the pieces that will help solve the puzzle of alcoholism are being discovered in laboratories around the world. Like cancer, alcoholism is actually many different diseases. What may be true of one type, may not be true of another. But the search, in a scientific fashion, has barely begun.

Who will become an alcoholic, and why, still remains largely a mystery. The seeds that grow into alcoholism seem to be nurtured by an almost unlimited number of factors. Many doctors and scientists who search for the answers to causes of this complex disease contribute to both the prevention of alcoholism and the treatment of those who have drunk too much, too often, and/or have a special body chemistry that makes them prone to the disease. In general, the medical profession does not claim to have a cure for alcoholism, but the picture is not all dark. Alcoholism can be arrested. Thousands of alcoholics return to normal living (through numerous and various kinds of help even though many mysteries remain unsolved).

"Alcoholism runs in families," is a statement that has long been expressed by many who belong to such families as well as by those who do not. Does it really? What do today's researchers know about the genetic factor in alcoholism?

At the Institute of Behavioral Genetics at the University of Colorado at Boulder, researchers are trying to find out more about predisposition to alcoholism. While the disease is recognized as psychological, social, environmental, and nutritional, genes do seem to play a part.

In experiments with mice, if one crosses a normal mouse with one that has been bred to develop a preference for alcohol over water, the offspring will be mixed. Some will prefer water; some will prefer alcohol. The differences in liver enzymes may be involved, but researchers do not know the entire story.

Genetic predisposition to alcoholism is being studied by many men and women. Dr. Donald Goodwin at Washington University in St. Louis, Missouri, is an especially important contributor in this area. He and his colleagues explored the role of genetic factors in alcoholism in one study by interviewing individuals who had been adopted. Some of these individuals had an alcoholic biological parent but were not raised by alcoholics. In comparison, people from broken homes who were raised by unrelated alcoholics were studied. It was found that having a biological parent who was an alcoholic predicted alcoholism in the offspring by a sixfold factor when compared with people raised by stepfathers who were alcoholic.

From this and other studies, Dr. Goodwin gives the following answer to the question, "Is alcoholism hereditary?" He believes that it appears established that alcoholism runs in families but that the mode of familiar transmission is still unknown even after a century of studies and speculation. A genetic factor may be involved. Or perhaps there is some neonatal factor, something that influences a newborn; or perhaps, there is some influence before the baby is born.

Recent research seems to confirm a clear-cut relationship between deformed babies and alcoholic mothers. It is also known that alcohol readily crosses the placenta and that alcohol consumed by a pregnant woman soon reaches the fetus. No one knows whether or not drinking during pregnancy might have an effect on the desire of the unborn to drink large amounts later in life. All that is known in this connection is that alcoholic mothers may give birth to deformed children in the rates of as many as 20 births per 100.

Children of alcoholics are usually exposed to alcoholic beverages more than children of social drinkers. Such an environment may be a "trigger" that influences development when a genetic predisposition is present. Or is the problem one of environment alone? Once more the old "nature vs. nurture" argument arises.

Some twin studies involved seven generations, and seemed to indicate that nature played a more important part than nurture. For example, in the study of identical twins, one could predict the development of alcoholism in a person who had an alcoholic parent even though there was no contact with that parent. In this study, it was felt that there was no bias. For example, there were no more environmental stresses, no special personality disorders, no other disorders that were out of the ordinary. The only special thing, or common factor, that seemed to characterize the offspring of the alcoholics was the abnormally high rate of alcoholism. The chance of developing the disease was four times as great.

Having established the probability of predisposition to alcoholism through the above and other studies, researchers are now trying to determine the answer to the question: What is being transmitted? This is assumed to have something to do with body chemistry, but no one knows exactly what. Does it fit into patterns of genetic inheritance known for eye color, curly hair, hair color, body height and shape, proteins in the blood, and the many other characteristics which are known to be transmitted through certain genetic patterns? Such research takes many years and much money.

You will not necessarily become an alcoholic just because other people in your family are or have been; this seems certain. The predisposition to other diseases, such as tuberculosis, runs in families, too, but this does not mean you will eventually suffer from them. In the case of alcohol, you have a choice about whether or not to drink. Knowing that there may be genetic predisposition could help you to avoid alcoholism and, while it does seem probable that genetic factors are involved with alcoholism, this does not mean that it applies to all types.

What part does one's social role play in the development of alcoholism? Here, too, much remains to be learned. At the University of Colorado, the effect of social position, social role, and social dissatisfaction is being tested on mice in relationship to alcohol preference. Conditions are set up so that there are environmental situations that produce a social hierarchy, with strong losers and winners. Picture a community of mice in which there is a strong, dominant male who punishes a "social loser" mouse by biting his hindquarters and tail. The tail becomes very sore and the "punished mouse" is very sick for several days. This kind of situation generates a social scale among the mice.

Scientists are searching to find what happens to the losers when they have an opportunity to "drop out" by drinking more alcohol than water. But this is just part of the total problem, and there must always be remembered that there is a big gap between mice and man.

In addition to learning from the above, similar

experiments are being made with different strains of mice to determine the interaction between the genetic and social roles. In the case of man, being a social loser may be a concept he has in his own mind. Since men are far more complicated than mice, one can begin to see how difficult it is to draw conclusions.

Many experimenters use strains of mice which have been bred to prefer alcohol to water, but mice do not become alcoholics. Miniature pigs do, so they are good stand-ins for humans in alcohol experiments. Dr. Russel V. Brown of the University of Missouri's Sinclair Comparative Medical Research Farm has been learning about the behavior of alcoholic pigs for several years. Each miniature, 120-pound pig was given a quart or more of vodka per day for a period of 1-1/2 years. Much like humans, they could neither walk nor stand when they were very drunk. Some grew sleepy, while others exhibited aggressive behavior. Much like humans, some pigs were heavier drinkers than others when allowed to drink all they wanted. And the pigs also showed withdrawal symptoms similar to those found in humans when the supply of alcohol was stopped abruptly. Several died in withdrawal.

From his studies with mice and pigs, Dr. Brown also believes that there may be a hereditary factor involved in alcoholism. Some pigs and some people seem to have body chemistry which makes them potential alcoholics, while others could never become alcoholics.

The pigs that died in withdrawal were carefully examined to try to gain more information about this process. Withdrawal is the subject of research for many scientists, and new ideas are replacing old. In recent experiments, it has been found that the body is constantly producing ethyl and methyl alcohol in small amounts and that the same enzyme system handles the breaking down of both kinds of alcohol. Research by Dr. Bernard Korol of the Veterans Administration Hospital in St. Louis, Missouri, has shown that the enzyme system has an affinity for breaking down ethyl alcohol at a rate of about 16 times that of destroying methyl alcohol. So when a person drinks a considerable amount of ethyl alcohol, the enzyme system is busy with this chemical, and the methyl alcohol is neglected. The methyl alcohol made by the body accumulates.

Only when the enzyme system is finished breaking down the ethyl alcohol does it turn to the methyl alcohol. The breakdown of the latter produces formaldehyde, as mentioned in an earlier chapter. Formaldehyde, which is a very toxic substance in the body, may be one of the major chemicals responsible for symptoms of withdrawal.

Other experiments on methyl and ethyl alcohol are being carried out by different researchers, including Dr. Edward Majchrowicz, a biochemist at the National Institute of Alcohol Abuse and Alcoholism. In one of his studies, volunteers drank a quart of bourbon or grain alcohol each day for as long as 2 weeks. Dr. Majchrowicz measured the amounts of ethyl and methyl alcohol in their blood at intervals during this period of time, and afterward. He found that a hangover began only after the levels of ethyl alcohol became quite low, freeing enzymes to attack the methyl alcohol that had built up in the body.

While the old hangover cure of having another drink may stop the breakdown of methyl alcohol temporarily, it must eventually be removed from the body. Dr. Majchrowicz is trying to find how methyl alcohol is produced in the body in the first place. He then hopes to find a way to stop its production. This would help considerably, not only with problems of hangovers, but with the dangerous situations of withdrawal.

What goes on in the brains of alcoholics during withdrawal? Dr. Milton Gross of the New York Downstate Medical Center is studying the quality and quantity of sleep of alcoholics undergoing detoxification. He believes that certain sleep abnormalities may persist as a part of prolonged withdrawal. During withdrawal, patients are irritable, anxious, restless, and have trouble falling asleep. When they do fall asleep, they awaken after short periods of time and frequently waken in a startled condition. There is a drop in slow wave sleep, or deep sleep and dreaming, or REM, sleep is increasing during withdrawal. In some cases, there is total sleeplessness.

Dr. Gross notes that when an alcoholic is given 6 days of intensive hospital care and remains in the hospital for several more weeks, normal sleep patterns return. Disturbed sleep patterns may cause some people to resume drinking after withdrawal if withdrawal is not really complete. Understanding what is happening to sleep patterns during withdrawal and afterward may help doctors to understand more about why alcoholics start drinking again.

Better understanding of what happens in the brain is a very important part of alcoholism research since the central nervous system may be severely damaged by heavy drinking. Even in early stages, loss of memory is common. The alcoholic blackout is a form of amnesia which has been studied scientifically only in recent years. Some people perform highly complicated acts while drunk and have little or no recollection of them.

Behavior problems and alcoholism have long been known to go together. Although the aggression that frequently goes with too much drinking is more readily tolerated than aggression by a sober person, it can be just as serious.

The approaches to research in the field of alcoholism are varied and spread through laboratories in far parts of the world. Just a very few have been mentioned in this chapter, but each one that supplies a bit of information helps in the understanding of the problem and helps those who treat its victims to stop the progress of the disease while they can still build on the real strengths and potentialities of their patients.

More basic research is needed to help in the fields of prevention and treatment. At the present time, funds are greatest in the area of treatment, but more basic research might make treatment easier and more effective.

Prevention of Alcoholism

Alcoholism may be a mysterious disease about which much needs to be learned, but almost everyone agrees that it is undesirable and much too prevalent.

Recently, a large group of young people, the JAYCEES, inaugurated a 3-year program known as OPERATION THRESHOLD. This program is aimed at responsible drinking, prevention of alcohol abuse, and alcoholism. Much as new attitudes have been encouraged in areas such as mental retardation and mental health, positive attitudes toward responsible drinking are to be encouraged. While the United States Jaycees are well aware of the fact that the decision to drink or not to drink is a personal, private decision, they believe that anyone choosing to drink has a responsibility not to destroy himself or society. This, they believe, in its broadest sense, is responsible drinking.

Youth programs in Operation Threshold are varied and extensive in approach. The many local Jaycee chapters are actively translating an urgent public health concern—alcohol abuse and alcoholism—into community action at the local level. The impact of 325,000 young men aged 18–36 in 6,400 chapters throughout the country may do much to foster a new national environment regarding use and misuse of alcohol.

Through local programs which promote a

basic awareness of alcohol problems and change in attitudes, community fact-finding programs, halfway house support, Drinking While Intoxicated (DWI) court schools, support of treatment and rehabilitation programs, and so on, Operation Threshold will cover a wide range of approaches to the problem of alcohol abuse and alcoholism.

Never before has a volunteer private-civic group undertaken such a large-scale program to reach people long before serious alcohol problems develop.

Perhaps one of the most exciting parts of Operation Threshold is the recognition by young people that the alcohol problem is a part of the overall drug problem.

Consider the following findings as reported in "Drug Use in America: Problem in Perspective," *The Second Report of the National Commission on Marijuana and Drug Abuse* which was published in 1973. The prevalence of alcohol problems in the United States reaches about ten percent, and there is a serious decrease in ability to function normally in about half of these people. But according to a national survey sponsored by the Commission, alcohol is regarded as a drug by only 39 percent of the adult population and by 34% of the youth population. Only seven percent of the people questioned mentioned alcoholism as a serious social problem. About 53% mentioned drugs as a serious social problem.

Certainly, education and/or awareness programs are needed. But in addition to this approach, the Commission's report emphasized that a major goal in prevention is emphasis of:

> ... alternative means of obtaining what users seek from drugs; means that are better for the user and better for society. The aim of the prevention policy should be to foster and instill the necessary skills for coping with the problems of living, particularly the life concerns of adolescents. Information about drugs and the disadvantages of their use should be incorporated into more general programs, stressing benefits in which drug consumption is largely inconsistent.

While information about drugs, including alcohol, is preferable to ignorance, knowledge alone is not likely to alter behavior. Individuals need to be helped in finding means of rational living rather than relying on drugs which deal with the unrealistic worlds. Operation Threshold, community groups, health agencies, and public service groups of many varieties may play an intelligent part in helping to achieve a reduction of the amount of alcoholism. While the goal of prevention is a tremendously broad one, the theme may be, RESPONSIBLE DRINKING BEHAVIOR LARGELY DEPENDS ON KNOWING HOW TO DRINK. Certainly, this is a step in the right direction.

The "drunk" is no longer a laughable character. Public drunkenness has long been considered humorous and the drunken scene in many plays, movies, and television shows still may bring some laughter from the audience. But if the scene showed a person ill with a disease other than alcoholism, the audience might feel empathy. Laughing at someone who, in real life, is on the downhill road to alcoholism is an immature way of dealing with a problem. Today, many young people are trying to make it clear to the world that alcoholism is not a joke and that public drunkenness is neither funny nor acceptable behavior.

Drinking patterns, as well as attitudes, play a part in the prevention challenge. For example, for many Americans, there is a pattern of social pressure to drink more and more. Hosts and hostesses could help by making nonalcoholic beverages available, by not urging people to drink more than they wish, and creating a free take-it-or-leave-it atmosphere. One is not apt to think of such a person as a drug pusher, but, in the true sense, alcohol is the only legal mind drug that may be obtained without a prescription. Even though its use may be beneficial in moderation, alcohol abuse is discouraged even by the alcoholic beverage industry.

When you look at an advertisement for whiskey, beer, wine—or any kind of alcoholic beverage—do you look at it objectively? Certainly, the positive side of drinking is made obvious, but unless one has a close relationship with an alcoholic or has suffered a personal loss because of someone's drunken driving, the fun side or the glamourous side is much more impressive. Occasionally, one sees an advertisement sponsored by the Licensed Beverage Industries, Inc., whose aim is to encourage favorable public opinion. While they urge responsible use of their products, vast sums of money are spent to encourage drinking of specific beverages and *much* smaller amounts to develop attitudes of sensible drinking.

For many people, any kind of drinking is considered immoral. While the children of most of these people abstain or drink little later in life, it has been noted that alcoholics are most likely to come from families where there is too much drinking or none at all. Social acceptance of those who drink little or not at all should be as genuine as social acceptance of people who do not drink coffee or tea. In North America, strong disapproval of drunkenness and use of wine in religious ceremonies is frequently cited as reasons for the low rate of alcoholism among Jews.

Cultural patterns, as they concern alcohol, are not completely understood. At the present time, there is not even complete agreement on the part played by the total amount of intake of alcohol. People who customarily drink with meals, such as the Italians, have long been thought to be relatively free of alcoholism. But according to one study by the Addiction Research Foundation of Canada, it reports that in 1970 in Italy there was a drinking population of 41,329,600 people 15 years and older. They consumed 858,325,350 litres of absolute alcohol during that year, or roughly 20-3/4 litres of absolute alcohol per person. A high rate of deaths from cirrhosis of the liver has been reported for a number of years. This rate is one considered in estimating the rate of alcoholism. In 1968, the Italian liver cirrhosis rate was 31.4 per 100,000 people. This rate is 3/4 of that for France. In the same year, the Italian excess drinking rate was reported as 8/9 of France.

In France, the problem of alcoholism is well recognized. Perhaps, the high rate is due to the habit of drinking many times throughout the day and to the beginning of alcohol consumption at an early age. Is the prevalence of alcoholism in a population related to availability and overall level of consumption? According to Jan De Lint and Wolfgang Schmidt who published the study, there is proportionately higher number of alcoholics as the per capita consumption of alcohol increases. In preventive approaches to the problem, they feel that social drinkers and alcoholics should not be considered separate groups or separate populations and that the overall consumption of alcohol should be rolled back throughout our society.

Children know about alcohol at an early age.

In fact, in one study in Glasgow, Scotland, researchers concluded that attitudes in drinking and alcohol gradually take shape from ages 6 to 10. Impact aiming at moderate drinking might be easier at that formative stage. Another study also reported in the *Journal,* published by the Addiction Research Foundation of Canada, notes that by early teen age, attitudes have already begun to harden and habits of drinking behavior are being established.

Drinking attitudes for a substantial number of young people begin in the home. The percentage of alcoholics from homes where drinking is forbidden *or* where drinking is irresponsible is abnormally high. For this reason, and as a result of other studies, groups such as the American Medical Association, the American School Health Association, and the National Council of Churches are encouraging parents to teach young people how to drink responsibly if they wish to drink at all.

Certainly, attitudes toward alcohol are influenced by religious beliefs and ethnic and cultural practices as well as by myths which claim that being able to "hold one's liquor" is a sign of virility. Most young people probably learn to drink as they assume adult roles, but only a small percentage abuse alcohol as a drug in rebellion to laws which they believe to be stupid, parents whom they wish to defy, or for other reasons.

Past experience has shown that the prevention of alcoholism cannot be accomplished by punitive methods or prohibition. Fear and guilt do not discourage drinking. Campaigns and slogans do not seem to help. But meaningful programs such as those which teach those who want to drink how to do so in a responsible way, drinking in a family setting, knowledge about kinds of alcoholic beverages and the effect they have on the body at various times, how much and when to drink may all be important and positive ways toward prevention.

Alcoholism Is Not Forever

Drunkenness has been called an overdose of a drug, and alcoholism is often referred to as a form of slow suicide because of its destructive effect on the human body. Certainly, alcholism is a progressive, destructive disease which can end in brain damage, numerous physical impairments, and eventually, in death. But it need not.

Early treatment is a very important asset in controlling alcoholism. Most people have difficulty in admitting that they have such a problem and do not go for help until the disease has progressed quite far. This is partly due to the fact that alcoholics have been treated for criminal offenses through the years. Moral stigma attached to alcoholism has been a great detriment to those who were aware of a growing problem with alcohol. For many years, alcoholism was "swept under the rug." Even today, doctors avoid writing alcoholism on death certificates.

While the American Hospital Association recognized alcoholism as a medical problem as far back as 1944, it is estimated that as many as 50% of the inpatients in any hospital have involvement with alcohol but are admitted under other categories such as digestive problems, nervous disorders, and so on. Frank diagnosis is encouraged, but many hospitals are afraid of being known as "drunk tanks" if they expand their alcoholism programs. So, even in today's world of growing awareness and concern with the treatment of alcoholism, there is important work to be done.

Treating alcoholism as a health problem permits prevention, early detection of the disease, or effective treatment and rehabilitation.

What is the cure for alcoholism? At the present time, the answer is "none." Perhaps, there will never be a cure that fits all cases since the disease is actually many diseases, but the importance of early treatment is present in all. Some doctors estimate that by treating people before they have destroyed their emotional resources and before the physical damage is too great, the rate of recovery could be as great as 80%. In many reports, the actual figure for rehabilitation is nearer 20%.

Treatment approaches vary according to the need. Often an alcoholic finds one kind of treatment more helpful than the other, but he may enter a program just because he happens to know about it rather than because it is the right one for him.

If one understands that part of the problem of alcoholism may be due to body chemistry, is it easier to consult a doctor? Alcohol has a highly addictive potential for some people, but since it is a socially accepted drug, the social drinkers and nondrinkers may tend to consider the abusers as suffering from a kind of moral weakness. Such attitudes discourage the seeking of treatment. Such attitudes keep the problem in the closet until it may be too late for help.

Today, the treatment of alcoholics takes place in mental hospitals, general hospitals, specialized alcohol clinics, community mental health centers, halfway houses, private doctors' offices, and in groups where there is no medical aid. The earliest treatment approach belongs to the latter type. It is Alcoholics Anonymous, or AA, which began in 1935 when two "hopeless alcoholics" found their way to sobriety. Today, this movement has spread around the world and has helped untold numbers of alcoholics to return to normal living without drinking. Some consider AA as the first group therapy program, for much is based on helping each other to refrain from alcoholic beverages.

What can you do to help solve the complex problem known as alcoholism? Since even the experts disagree on causes, prevention methods, treatment methods, and so forth, one tends to be somewhat bewildered. But there is one thing on which the experts do agree and that is the fact that alcoholism is not related to willful misconduct. Whether conditioning is involved, whether heredity is an important part are all fields for the experts to explore. But the dependency on alcohol is widespread, and individuals by the millions need treatment.

You can help by encouraging a change in public attitude, by knowing what research is being done and what needs to be done, and by making people aware that this problem effects every individual, whether or not he cares.

Suggestions
for Further
Reading

Bacon, Margaret, and Jones, Mary Brush, *Teen-age Drinking.* New York, Thomas Y. Crowell, 1968.

Blanes, Howard T., *The Personality of the Alcoholic: Guises of Dependency.* New York, Harper & Row, 1968.

Block, Marvin A., M.D., *Alcoholism, Its Facets and Phases.* New York, John Day Co., 1962, 1965.

——, *Alcohol and Alcoholism: Drinking and Dependence.* Belmont, Calif., Wadsworth Pub., 1970.

Brenner, Joseph H., Coles, Robert, and Meagher, Dumot, *Drugs and Youth.* New York, Liveright Publishing Corp., 1970.

Cahalan, Don, *Problem Drinkers.* San Francisco, Calif., Josey Bass, 1970.

——, *American Drinking Practices.* New Brunswick, N.J., Rutgers Center of Alcohol Studies, 1969.

Cahn, Sydney, *The Treatment of Alcoholics.* New York, Oxford University Press, 1970.

——, *The Treatment of Alcoholics; An Evaluative Study.* New York, Oxford University Press, 1970.

Carroll, Charles R., *Alcohol: Use, Non-Use, and Abuse.* Dubuque, Iowa, William C. Brown, 1970.

Caruba, Rebecca, *Cooking with Wine and High Spirits.* New York, Crown Publishers, 1963.

Chafetz, Morris E., Blane, Howard T., and Hill, Marjorie J., *Frontiers of Alcoholism.* New York, Science House, 1970.

————, and Demone, Harold W., *Alcoholism and Society.* New York, Oxford University Press, 1962.

Chidsey, Donald Barr, *On and Off the Wagon: A Sober Analysis of the Temperance Movement from the Pilgrims Through Prohibition.* New York, Cowles Book Co., Inc., 1969.

————, *Drug Use in America: Problem in Perspective.* Second Report of the National Commission on Marijuana and Drug Abuse; Washington, D.C., Superintendent of Documents, U.S. Government Printing Office, 1973.

Coffey, Timothy, *Gin Street.* New Brunswick, N.J., Rutgers Center for Alcohol Studies.

Fort, Joel, *Alcohol: Our Biggest Drug Problem.* New York, McGraw-Hill Book Co., 1973.

Grossman, Harold J., *Grossman's Guide to Wines, Spirits, and Beers.* New York, Charles Scribner's Sons, 1964.

Greenberg, Leon A., Ed., *Studies of Congeners in Alcoholic Beverages.* New Brunswick, N.J., Rutgers Center of Alcohol Studies, 1970.

Jones, Kenneth, L., et al. *Drugs: Alcohol and Tobacco.* New York, Harper & Row, 1970.

Kalant, Harold, and Kalant, Oriana Josseau, *Drugs, Society and Personal Choice.* Ontario, Canada, Paperbacks, Addiction Research Foundation, 1971.

Keller, Mark, and McCormick, Mairi, *A Dictionary of Words About Alcohol.* New Brunswick, N.J., Rutgers Center of Alcohol Studies, 1968.

Layton, T. A., *Wines and Chateaux of the Loire.* London, Cassell and Company, Ltd. 1967.

Marrison, L. W., *Wines and Spirits.* Baltimore, Md., Penguin Books, 1970.

McClelland, David; Davis, William; Kalin, Rudolf, and Wanner, Eric, *The Drinking Man: Alcohol and Human Motivation.* New York, The Free Press, 1973.

Mello, Nancy K., and Mendelson, Jack H., Ed., *Recent Advances in Studies of Alcoholism.* An Interdisciplinary Symposium; Washington, D.C., U. S. Government Printing Office, 1971.

Muir, Augustus, Ed., *How to Choose and Enjoy Wine.* New York, Crown Publishers, 1972.

Plaut, Thomas F. A., and the Cooperative Commission on the Study of Alcoholism, *Alcohol Problems: A Report to the Nation.* New York, Oxford University Press, 1967.

Popham, R. E., Ed., *Alcohol and Alcoholism.* Toronto, University of Toronto Press, 1970.

Roach, Mary K., et al, Ed., *Biological Aspects of Alcohol.* Austin, Texas, University of Texas Press, 1971.

Roueche, Berton, *Alcohol: The Neutral Spirit.* New York, Little, Brown and Co., 1960; Berkeley Medallion Edition, 1971.

Simon, André L., *Encyclopedia of Wine.* New York, Quadrangle Books, Inc., 1973.

Tritton, S. M., *Guide to Better Wine and Beer Making for Beginners.* New York, Dover Publications, 1969.

Waldo, Myra, *The Pleasures of Wine: A Guide to Wines of the World.* New York, Crowell-Collier Pub. Co., 1963.

Wallgreen, Henrick, and Herbert Barry III, *Actions of Alcohol.* 2 vol., New York, American Elsevier Pub. Co., 1971.

Wilkinson, Rupert, *The Prevention of Drinking Problems: Alcohol Control and Cultural Influences.* New York, Oxford University Press, 1970.

Waugh, Alec, *Wines and Spirits.* Foods of the World Series. New York, Time-Life Pub. Co., 1968.

Younger, William, *Gods, Men, and Wine.* Cleveland, Ohio, World Publishing Company, 1966.

Index